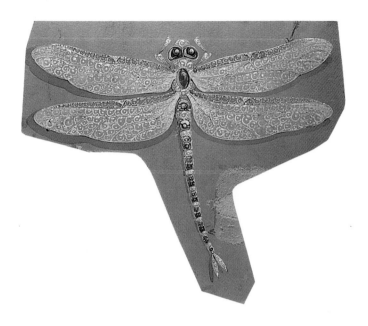

TIFFANY'S 150 YEARS

John Loring

Introduction by Louis Auchincloss

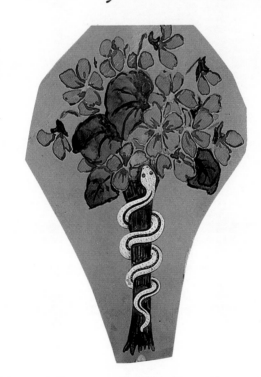

DOUBLEDAY & COMPANY, INC.

Garden City, New York

1987

Acknowledgments

Tiffany & Co. gratefully acknowledges the exceptional contributions of Yone Akiyama, Tiffany's Associate Design Director, for her role as director of photography; Natasha Kuzmanovic and Rachel Mullen for their assistance in research; and Janet Zapata, Tiffany's Archivist, for her many discoveries in public and private collections and in Tiffany's own archives that have shed so much light on our history.

Also by John Loring:

TIFFANY TASTE
THE NEW TIFFANY TABLE SETTINGS (with Henry B. Platt)

Designed by Jean-Claude Suarès

Library of Congress Cataloging-in-Publication Data

Loring, John.
   Tiffany's 150 years.

   Tiffany and Company.   2. Decoration and ornament—United States.   I. Title.
NK7398.T5L67   1987   338.7'61745'097471   87-3319
ISBN: 0-385-24252-2

PAGES 2–3
Tiffany Scrapbook from the 1880s

Scrapbook from the 1800s of Tiffany designs for perfume vials, a cane handle, diamond tiaras, and other jewels on a jeweler's workbench at Tiffany's 727 Fifth Avenue store. The jeweler's bench and tools have changed little since the 1880s.

TABLE OF CONTENTS

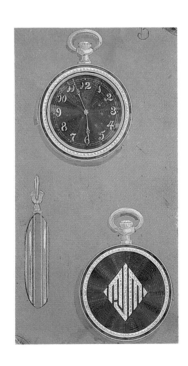

Dear Tiffany

A thing of beauty
is a joy *forever*
that is why the lustre
of the art of Tiffany's
remains undimmed.

For 150 years your name
has stood for beauty
            style
            quality
        and constancy
you have brightened our faces
        with your jewelry
illuminated our homes
        with your lamps
brought a glow to our
        tables with your silver
given distinction to our
            lives
you certainly have to mine by
inviting me to breakfast—how many
can say they've had coffee and
croissants at Tiffany's—a memory
I shall always cherish.

Happy Birthday, dear T.,
with love—but also with envy,
for after 150 years you don't
have a wrinkle—but then, class
doesn't age!

Your devoted friend,

Audrey Hepburn

iffany's 150 Years DOCUMENTS A CENTURY AND A HALF OF THE MARRIAGE OF WEALTH AND decorative arts in America.

Since 1837 Tiffany & Co. has provided successful Americans with jewels for their celebrations, trophies for their sports events, commemorative objects for their milestones, and ornaments for their desks and dining tables. It has also provided every sort of tribute to their loved ones, their yachts, their horses, their battles, their governments, and, of course, their money. And Tiffany's has succeeded throughout its one hundred and fifty years in translating the enthusiasms of its clientele into decorative artworks of consistent and exemplary merit.

Tiffany's 150 Years documents the institution's history from September 21, 1837, when Charles Louis Tiffany opened the doors of a small "fancy goods" and stationery store at 259 Broadway in New York in the midst of bank failures and the "Panic of 1837," to its present position as a world arbiter of quality in the appurtenances of luxury.

Tiffany's has maintained an extraordinarily complete archive; and *Tiffany's 150 Years* illustrates the company's history with photos and drawings of the most historic and sumptuous objects produced by its great designers, jewelers, and silversmiths.

More than this, *Tiffany's 150 Years* is a "social" history; its illustrations were selected for their human as well as graphic interest. Their aim is to illustrate the evolution of American society as seen through the eyes of its preeminent purveyor of luxuries. Included are objects as diverse as the Super Bowl Trophy and the Empress Eugénie's jewels. There are Tiffany's great yachting and racing trophies, the Goelet Cup and Belmont Cup; the sterling silver Tiffany bicycle commissioned for Lillian Russell; the silver filigree horse and carriage P. T. Barnum ordered for the wedding of Tom Thumb; the pearl necklace and bracelets Abraham Lincoln gave Mary Todd Lincoln; Gypsy Rose Lee's fire opals; and the Lyndon Johnson White House china.

Photographs of Tiffany stores' interiors and exteriors show Tiffany's expansion as it moved farther and farther uptown with the growth of New York. (The first shop on Broadway, next to A. T. Stewart's, and the larger cast-iron Tiffany building at 550 Broadway are only documented in drawings, but the great Tiffany emporium at Union Square and Sixteenth Street and Stanford White's Italianate Tiffany palace on Fifth Avenue at Thirty-seventh Street, as well as Tiffany's nineteenth-century London and Paris branches, are all documented by excellent period photographs.)

Supporting illustrations in *Tiffany's 150 Years* show the rich and celebrated in their jewels; the proud with their trophies; models and studies for such famous objects as the Magnolia Vase and the Adams Vase (both in the Metropolitan Museum of Art); illustrations from the covers of Tiffany catalogues of one hundred years ago; the Tiffany invitation to the dedication of the Statue of Liberty; a letter from Cyrus Field authenticating the first transatlantic telegraph cable that Charles Tiffany cut up and sold in souvenir lengths at untold profit; and a letter from August Belmont inviting members of the Tiffany Design Department to visit his stable on Long Island to sketch his three favorite horses for the Belmont Cup.

Twenty-three royal houses were counted among Tiffany's clients by the end of the nineteenth century. They included Queen Victoria of England, the Czar and Czarina of Russia, the Shah of Persia, the Khedive of Egypt, the Emperor of Brazil, and the kings of Italy, Denmark, Belgium, and Greece; and they were joined by a veritable army of celebrities: Jenny Lind, Mark Twain, J. P. Morgan, General Sherman, Nevada's "Silver Bonanza King" John Mackay, Marcel Proust, the Astors, the Goulds, the Belmonts, Lincoln, Barnum, the U.S. Congress, the U.S. Army and Navy, and successive presidents of the United States.

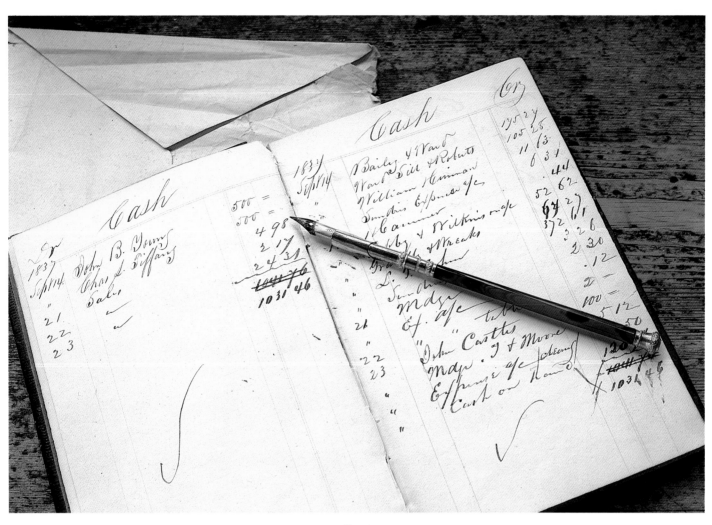

Tiffany's First Cash Book

In the midst of the financial "Panic of 1837," Charles L. Tiffany and John P. Young, with a loan of $1,000 from Tiffany's father, opened a "Stationery and Dry Goods" store in lower Manhattan at 259 Broadway. The original cash book records the first day's sales of $4.98.

Tiffany Store at 259 Broadway, 1837–1841

In 1837 Charles L. Tiffany and John P. Young opened their new business at 259 Broadway in the heart of the New York shopping district and next door to another of America's greatest merchants, Alexander Turner Stewart.

By the turn of the century the firm had won scores of gold medals at the great world's fairs and "universal expositions" which showcased the lush inventions of the Industrial Revolution and the Arts and Crafts Movement.

However, in 1837, New York City was not a capital of quality and style and Tiffany's future was not assured. Although gifted with a sense of showmanship, a sound New Englander's head for business, and a penchant for the finer things of life, the young Tiffany found himself in a world of little aesthetic sensitivity. His wealthy clients, unsure of their new fortunes, demanded either the academic imitation of past styles characteristic of the Victorian era, or sentimental copies of nature's bounty. As a result, Tiffany's showrooms held their share of neo-medieval armors, marble sea nymphs, bronze beasts, and an idiosyncratic array of the inhabitants of souks, jungles, dens, and barnyards.

Charles Tiffany was equal to any prince of commerce of his day. He catered to his clients' unruly tastes, but he also delighted and surprised them with ideas of his own. He dazzled everyone by bringing home the diamonds of deposed French Empress Eugénie, and he captured and displayed the most extraordinary diamond in America, the great 128.51-carat canary yellow Tiffany Diamond.

The profits from such enterprises were enormous, and Tiffany wisely reinvested his thriving fortune in his business to improve his store and the quality of merchandise it offered. Fifty years after its founding, it was estimated that Tiffany's vaults held over forty million dollars in gemstones, a staggering sum in nineteenth-century New York.

Tiffany occasionally indulged his genius for promotion in projects of dubious aesthetic quality that were nonetheless triumphs of American marketing. When his friend and fellow promoter P. T. Barnum was obliged to destroy a man-killing elephant from his circus, Tiffany bought the elephant's hide and put it on display to promote a collection of leather goods for which it would serve as raw material. The police had to be called in to control the mob of buyers.

A broken cable does not represent an obvious marketing opportunity to most jewelers; but Charles Tiffany in 1858 bought miles of Cyrus Field's first transatlantic telegraph cable and resold it in two-inch sections to clamoring crowds at enormous profit.

Not only a promoter, Tiffany also had an infallible sense of quality and style. He recognized in the American silversmith John C. Moore a partner whose expertise could secure Tiffany's position as the world's leading silver maker. And in Moore's son, Edward C. Moore, he recognized a genius who would help Tiffany lead American decorative arts out of the doldrums of Victorianism into the twentieth century.

In 1878 Tiffany's received the Grand Prix and a gold medal at the Exposition Universelle in Paris for their magnificent silverware, and Charles Tiffany was given the Legion of Honor. All this to the voiced dismay of the English, who lamented in the London *Spectator*, "We confess we were surprised and ashamed to find that a New York firm, Tiffany & Co., had beaten the old country and the old world in domestic silver plate."

Fifteen years later, at the 1893 World's Columbian Exposition in Chicago, Tiffany's Magnolia Vase, Viking Bowl, and other masterpieces of American design and craftsmanship brought the company no fewer than fifty-six medals. Tiffany capitalized on Moore's fertile imagination; although he never had the title, Moore was unquestionably Tiffany's first "design director."

Moore put together a then unique collection (which he eventually gave to the Metropolitan Museum) of decorative arts from Europe, the Orient, and the Middle East to serve as inspiration for Tiffany's Product Design Department. And it was he who decreed that design should not be tied to past forms, but should perpetually evolve, be elegant and modern.

Moore's designs, such as "Audubon" silver flatware, first introduced in 1871, are still bestsellers one hundred and sixteen years later, a monument to the enduring standard of design at Tiffany's.

It was Moore who introduced Charles Tiffany's son (and Tiffany & Co.'s first official design director), Louis Comfort Tiffany, to the sensuous curving forms and rich iridescent surfaces of Classical and Islamic glasswares that so strongly influenced his work. Moore also made him aware of the emerging Arts and Crafts Movement of which the junior Tiffany was to become a recognized world leader.

Louis Comfort Tiffany's achievements and the world fame he brought to the Tiffany name are common knowledge. Tiffany looked on his creative life as "a quest for beauty," and no success was denied him in that quest. Art Nouveau or "the Tiffany style," as it was popularly called, with its relentless use of eccentric curves and parabolic arches, its insets and lilies, its verdigrised and gilded surfaces, may have little relevance today in our technological world, but no one can look with indifference at this triumph of imagination that forever transformed the history of world design.

By the time Louis Comfort Tiffany died in 1933, the world had been altered by the harsh realities of life in the era following World War I.

Tiffany's second design director, Van Day Truex, was invited to join the company in 1955 by the new owner, Walter Hoving. Under Truex, formerly president of the Parsons School of Design, Tiffany's took a quantum leap to the suave surfaces and pared-down forms that are the company's trademark. Truex was convinced, like Edward Moore and Louis Tiffany before him, that nature's often hidden structure is the origin of the best design.

Mr. Hoving, who also owned Bonwit Teller next door, brought over Bonwit's genius of window display, Gene Moore, who received but one instruction: "Make the windows beautiful." With wit and artistry, that is exactly what he did.

In 1956 Walter Hoving brought from France the brilliant Jean Schlumberger, the Cellini of the modern age. Schlumberger's splendid rococo birds sitting on huge gemstones, emeralds and diamonds "stitched" and tied with gold strings, and jewel-studded sea creatures caused astonishment and delight.

In 1974 Hoving and Henry B. Platt, Tiffany's president, lured the gifted Elsa Peretti to Tiffany's. Her sensual and pure interpretations of popular symbols are masterpieces of modern design.

"Good design is good business" has always been Tiffany's motto. Walter Hoving practiced it with flair.

In April 1979 Van Day Truex died and I succeeded him as design director. In 1981 Pablo Picasso's youngest daughter, Paloma, joined Tiffany's design team. Her boldly colored abstract designs display great style and smartly harnessed energy.

Tiffany's creed, from Charles Tiffany to the present ownership led by William Chaney, has been to avoid passing fashions and to concentrate on lasting quality. *Tiffany's 150 Years* is the culmination of the "Tiffany Taste"—for objects of beauty and style which bring glamour to life's rituals and celebrations.

John Loring

Diamond Salesroom, 1879

Published in
1879, this print of Tiffany's
diamond salesroom at the
Union Square store illustrated
the dazzling array of
merchandise displayed in the
firm's specially designed
airtight cases.

*Tiffany Store at 550 Broadway,
1853–1870*

Following New
York's move north, Tiffany's
moved in 1853 to 550
Broadway, where it
remainded until 1870.

I N THE WINTER OF 1840, JUST THREE YEARS AFTER CHARLES TIFFANY AND JOHN P. YOUNG HAD SET UP A stationery and "fancy goods" store on Broadway facing City Hall Park, Mr. and Mrs. Henry Brevoort gave what fashionable ex-mayor and conscientious diarist Philip Hone described as a *bal costumé, costumé à la rigeur,* in their fine new mansion on Ninth Street, "better calculated for such a display than any other in the city." "Everyone appeared as someone else, the dresses being generally new, some of them superbly ornamented with gold, silver and jewelry." Hone himself went as Cardinal Wolsey. If he failed to astonish the folk with his magnificence, he records, then he had spent his money in vain for scarlet marino and other trappings "to decorate the burly person of the haughty churchman."

But the evening was in part marred for the former mayor by the presence of a reporter, clad as a knight in armor, from James Gordon Bennett's "infamous penny paper," the *Herald.* Bennett, it turned out, had called upon the millionaire son of a boon companion of Washington Irving, Mr. Brevoort, who had made a fortune working for John Jacob Astor in the fur trade, to obtain a bid for his newspaperman. The bid was granted only in the hope that the favor might soften the customary slander of the *Herald*'s social notes. Hone was outraged at this pressure from "a newspaper reformer striving to sow the seeds of discontent in an unruly population." Had he been able to look into the future, he would have no doubt been dismayed to learn that there would be hostesses one fine day, and of old and distinguished families too, who, far from knuckling under to such blackmail, would actually engage press agents to give wider coverage to their entertainments.

New York society had emerged from the restraints and disciplines of the eighteenth century; it had survived the threatened democratic upheavals of the Jacksonian era, and it was now embarking on the course that would take it ultimately to the extravagances of the Mauve Decade and the Edwardian Age. Tiffany & Co. was to play an important role in this story, in some ways analogous to that of our Supreme Court in the development of constitutional law. One of the most vital functions of that tribunal is to act as a brake on social reform, even necessary reform, to keep it from coming too fast. Liberal opinion is inclined to want too much too soon, and time is needed for the appropriate legislation to be worked out. Yet when that happens, and the court moderates or even reverses its earlier opinions, there still remains about it an aura of stability that lends force and dignity to the concept of law. Similarly Tiffany & Co. has achieved its position in the history of American taste by refusing to give in to every new fad and fancy for the sake of a fast buck, yet has always been willing to adapt itself in the long run to any fundamental change in manners.

The people who dressed up as Mary Stuart or Bothwell for the Brevoorts made up the quiet, naïve, and conservative society that the young Edith Wharton was to know in its final phase, just after the Civil War, and to dub the Age of Innocence. The hero's mother in her novel of that name lives with her son and daughter in a brownstone on West Twenty-eighth Street that must have dated from the 1850s:

"An upper floor was dedicated to Newland, and the two women squeezed themselves into narrower quarters below. In an unclouded harmony of tastes and interests they cultivated ferns in Wardian cases, made macramé lace and wool embroidery on linen, collected American revolutionary glazed ware, subscribed to 'Good Words' and read Ouida's novels for the sake of the Italian atmosphere."

The "sturdy English and the rubicund and heavier Dutch" of antebellum New York, as Mrs. Wharton put it, "had mingled to produce a prosperous, prudent and yet lavish society," and one that was quite ready for such emporiums as Tiffany's and his neighbor on Broadway, Alexander Turner Stewart's, ready to be titillated and tempted, but still suspicious, cautious, with a strong underpinning of the puritan.

The diarist George Templeton Strong, then a young lawyer employed in drafting wills for many of its

Bennett Candelabrum

This thirty-five-inch-high, five-hundred-ounce candelabrum with American Indian motifs, photographed in the Tiffany display at the Paris International Exposition of 1878, was made for James Gordon Bennett, Jr., publisher of the New York *Herald*, to commemorate a yacht-racing victory. The most spectacular profligate of the Gilded Age, Bennett reputedly commanded his yachts in the style of Captain Bligh. One newspaper reviewer concluded that the Indian waving a scalp at the top of the candelabrum indicated the precise way in which Bennett himself would have liked to triumph over even his friendliest opponents.

*A Tiffany Union Square Store
Display Window*

The quality, variety, and abundance of luxury items seen in this Tiffany window display of the late nineteenth century corroborate the high praise that Tiffany & Co. received on opening its new Union Square premises in 1870. Hailed as the largest and most magnificent jewelry palace in the world, Tiffany's new treasure house was filled with sumptuous merchandise made in its own workshops as well as imported from every corner of the globe.

members, records on the last day of 1845: "Spent the morning in a general investigation of Tiffany & Young's stock of gimcrackery and the selection of divers New Year's presents therefrom."

Three years later, harassed to fit his income to his swelling commitments, Strong finds Tiffany's almost diabolically tempting:

"I experience today a gloomy, superstitious foreboding of duns, a mournful presentiment of a bank account pumped dry, and impertinent creditors to be bullied or dodged. Perhaps it's because I went into Tiffany's with Ellen this morning and saw a great many things I wanted but could not afford to buy. But Ellen's a heroine. The way she turned away her eyes from beholding vanity and calmly defied the insinuating attacks of a whole bevy of most eloquent and argumentative salesmen, conceded that various gimcracks were beautiful, were immensely cheap and would suit her exactly, but concluded with the avowal that she should not buy them or let me buy them, was delightful to behold. It reminded me of the superhuman firmness of some Christian matron of the times of Diocletian quietly repelling all the entreaties and persuasions of a whole gang of Priests of Jupiter-Flamens and Arch Flamens, heorically holding fast her faith and refusing to burn incense on any terms before any heathen deity whatever."

By Christmas of 1857 Strong was secure enough financially to be able to buy his beloved Ellen a brooch from Tiffany's without commenting on the store's unprincipled threats to his moral well-being. But with the advent of the Civil War the critical note reappears in the diary. Strong now wonders when the crushing calamity that has struck the nation will become real and personal to *all* the population, "when there shall be no more long trains of carriages all along Fifth Avenue bound for Central Park, when the wives and daughters of contractors shall cease to crowd Stewart's and Tiffany's."

The public image of a luxury store is always going to invite slurs in wartime, particularly when the profiteers become its regular customers. Tiffany's managed to give a more patriotic luster to its name by offering the public models of French swords and rifles, gold epaulets, cap ornaments, and navy laces, displayed under the legend: "Goods forwarded to all parts of loyal states." And after Appomattox there was, of course, a lively business in commemorative swords and medals. During the First World War, more seriously, Tiffany's converted a part of its silver factory in New Jersey to the production of surgical instruments, and in the Second World War its craftsmen were able to manufacture by hand new baffles for cooling engines in time to replace Colonel James Doolittle's defective ones and make possible his daring raid on Tokyo. But essentially, in the dark days of war Tiffany products were always going to seem what Strong called gimcrackery. The problem was neatly put in a cartoon of Helen Hokinson's in *The New Yorker* in 1942, depicting one of her plump, darling, ever-hopeful, and wistfully trusting middle-aged ladies exclaiming to a nonplussed salesman: "But there must be something in Tiffany's a young ensign can use on a minesweeper!"

Charles Lewis Tiffany, the founder of the store and its proprietor for sixty-five years (a period that almost exactly coincided with the reign of Queen Victoria) was the greatest merchant of his day. If he was known as the "King of Diamonds," his less famous partner, the designer Edward C. Moore, should have been known as the "King of Silver." Their steadily expanding business moved uptown from lower Broadway to Prince Street in 1854, and again in 1870 to a much larger edifice on Union Square with a cast-iron façade painted in no-nonsense drab. After Tiffany's death in 1902 the store moved twice more, first in 1905 to the Venetian palazzo (now, alas, defaced) that McKim, Mead & White designed for it on Fifth Avenue and Thirty-seventh Street, and finally in 1940 to its present site, a fine example of American Art Deco architecture by Cross & Cross.

Charles Tiffany came of modest but secure colonial stock; his grandfather had been a farmer in Massachusetts and his father the owner of a textile mill in Connecticut. They were upright, conscientious men, and Charles in his long business career never descended to the financial chicanery so common to the age. When he became rich, as he did, even by "robber baron standards," he continued to live simply, at least by Vanderbilt standards. He showed no tendency to be dazzled by the strutting of Fifth Avenue and Newport. Yet he knew that social world backward and forward; he knew the parvenus as well as the old families, and he was in an excellent position to moderate the exuberance of their tastes.

But not altogether. Nobody could have. The first two decades after the Civil War were marked by an uncontrollable ebullience. The carnage was over, and the West not yet exploited; expansion in commerce and industry seemed limitless. The national centennial was splashily celebrated in Philadelphia, and in New York, which proclaimed that the arts, too, must have their share in the general bonanza, the great cultural institutions: the Metropolitan Museum of Art, the American Museum of Natural History, the Lenox Library were founded. It is perhaps in commemorative silver and gold that the epoch is best represented; precious metal beaten into muscular forms seemed best adapted to express so much vigor and brawn.

Tiffany's greatest piece of the period was the William Cullen Bryant Vase, celebrating the life and works of that distinguished poet and citizen, and it is fortunate that the committee of patrons rejected, after due consideration, the runner-up design. This called for corner panels at the sub-base which would contain, in delicately wrought *relievo,* subjects from the poet's minor poems. "There the white-footed deer will stoop to crop the broken sprays; there shall the small mosquito float, nor angry hand shall rise to brush his wing."

Among Tiffany's most publicized pieces of this era was the testimonial to the Geneva arbitrators of the American claims for the depredations to commerce wrought by the Confederate cruiser *Alabama,* built in Liverpool in defiance of international law. The set included a vase, a candelabrum, and two wine coolers. On one cooler Agriculture displayed her plowshare and sheaf of wheat; on the other Commerce held up her anchor and meridional globe, both now happily compensated for the ravages of the Southern raider.

A more peaceful marine note was struck by two trophies: the Cape May Challenge cup whose stem supported two walrus heads with long tusks extending down to penetrate the base, and the Goelet Fortuna cup showing the genius of wind sporting with a very naked Nereid in the briny deep. But the triumph of realism came in 1879 in a candelabrum made for James Gordon Bennett, grown almost responsible since the Brevoort ball, which contrasted two Indians, symbols of War and Peace, one placidly paddling a canoe, while the other pranced in a savage jig, brandishing above his head the bloody trophy of his victory.

There were signs, however, of an amelioration of taste. In 1879 the *Daily National Hotel Reporter* related that the private dining rooms of the Hotel Windsor in Saratoga were supplied with Tiffany dinner cards and "tasteful menus which may be the vehicles for some bit of pleasantry or sentiment." It was even becoming common, the columnist observes, for such objects of American design to be seen on the dining room tables of the *haut monde* in Paris.

By 1883 Tiffany's was able to put out a release that took a strong stand for curbing exuberance in engraved cards and stationery in the interests of good taste:

"Some ladies' notepaper is brightly decorated. Among the designs are landscapes, birds, cats, dogs, butterflies, humorous figures, days of the week, names of prominent summer resorts. But such fancy stationery is little used except for the western and out-of-town trade. The illuminated papers are rather shunned by ladies of fashion and quiet good taste. Crests and initials are not as popular as they have been."

And where calling cards were concerned, the most ancient family rules were invoked:

"A young lady does not have a separate card until after her first season in society. Her name previous to that time is always engraved beneath that of her mother's. If there are more than one daughter 'Misses' is used."

Tiffany's indeed was assuming the role of a clearinghouse of good manners and taste. A fictional dialogue in *Puck* in 1887 between a Mrs. and Miss "Carlton-Pell" reveals their plan to go to Tiffany's not so much to buy a wedding present for an engaged young lady of their acquaintance as to discover what their friends are sending her. And a suburban columnist of the same era gave the ultimate sanction to a ruby ring observed at Tiffany's: "What a wonderful God who can put such a deep red color into a stone!"

The society created by the explosion of business development after the Civil War was, at least in its early stages, a fairly crude and pushing one, exemplified by the story of the oil tycoon who slammed his fist down on the desk of a European hotel manager and announced: "My wife likes the best and plenty of it!" But it is easy to overdo this aspect of the newly rich, as did John Armstrong Chanler in his book of savage satirical sonnets, *Scorpio*, when he thus delineated the "Diamond Horseshoe" of the Metropolitan Opera House:

> A fecund sight for a philosopher—
> Rich as Golconda's mine in lessons rare—
> That gem-bedizened horseshoe at the opera,
> Replete with costly hags and matrons fair!
> His votaresses doth Mammon there array,
> His Amazonian phalanx dread to face!
> To Mammon there do they their homage pay,
> Spangled with jewels, satins, silks and lace,
> Crones whose old bosoms within their corsets creak,
> Beldames whose slightest glance would fright a horse,
> Ghouls, when they speak one hears the grave mole squeak,
> Their escorts parvenus of features coarse.
> O rich array of luxury and vice,
> But spite of them the music's very nice.

It must be remembered that the parvenus did not arrive in a single body; they had to penetrate an older and more distinguished society that was already there. William B. Astor married the daughter of General John Armstrong and his son a Schermerhorn; Mrs. Ogden Mills, wife of a California Gold Rush millionaire, was born a Livingston of the Hudson Valley patroon family; Lilia Vanderbilt became the wife of W. Seward Webb, a grandson of George Washington's aide-de-camp and private secretary, and her niece became duchess of Marlborough. The integrated society that reached its pinnacle of conspicuous consumption in the 1890s and early 1900s was a complex blend of discipline and greed, of sybarites and puritans, of worldly cynics and devout simpletons. And as this was the society that patronized Tiffany's in the heyday of its pre-Walter Hoving history, that bought its jewelry, silverware, and porcelain there, that had its stationery, calling cards, and invitations engraved there, that, in short, adopted the store as more its shrine than Saint Bartholomew's itself, it merits some attention here.

Perhaps the most striking characteristic of this society, in contrast to its counterparts in London or Paris, was the near total absence of intellectuals or statesmen. It was made up of businessmen (I use the term to include financiers and brokers) and their families or heirs, with a goodly sprinkling of lawyers and (unlike

London) an occasional doctor (no dentists). It was also unleavened by artists. Mrs. Winthrop Chanler, writing of New York in the Mauve Decade, observed that the so-called Four Hundred would have "fled in a body from a painter, a musician or a clever Frenchman," and Edith Wharton in her memoirs tells of dining with a rich and fashionable cousin at a party that her hostess had described to a fellow guest as "rather Bohemian, I'm afraid" and deciding ruefully, after looking down the table, that the gathering had been so downgraded because it contained herself and the New York correspondent of the London *Times*!

I cannot resist inserting here Mrs. Chanler's description of the lady I suspect to have been Mrs. Wharton's hostess:

"Mrs. William B. Astor was the acknowledged leader [of New York society]. She always sat on the right of the host when she went to dinner parties; she wore a black wig and a great many jewels; she had pleasant, cordial manners and unaffectedly enjoyed her undisputed position."

But if Mrs. Chanler was a disillusioned Prospero, there were fortunately Mirandas to find the society that Tiffany served a "brave new world." Such a one was twenty-one-year-old Florence Adele Sloane, lovely granddaughter of William Henry Vanderbilt, who, although still unmarried, had her own separate listing in Ward McAllister's Four Hundred. In 1893 she did not find the pace of life in Newport in the least stultifying as these excerpts from her diary show:

"I have not got the blues at all this year; on the contrary, I am in excellent spirits. It is great fun seeing everyone and quite exciting. . . . Baron Fallon told me the other night that I was the most clever girl he had ever spoken to and a lot of other silly things. . . . The Englishman, Mr. Harrison, talked to me all the afternoon on the Gerry's yacht. . . . Aunt Alva gave me a big luncheon two days ago. No description can possibly give one an idea of how marvellously beautiful it [Marble House] is. . . . Aunt Jessie had a big dinner of twenty-four last night, and I enjoyed it very much. . . . I have been going out the whole time these last few days, lunches, dinners, tennis in the mornings, polo or golf in the afternoon. The dance here Monday night was one of the jolliest I have ever been to. We never got to bed until twenty-five minutes before six."

And when, a year later, she became engaged to James Burden, it is pleasant to record that there was only ecstasy as the Tiffany gifts came pouring in:

"My wedding presents are beginning to come in faster and faster, over thirty now. The ones from Papa and Mamma and Uncle Corneil [Vanderbilt] and Aunt Alice have completely taken away my breath. Papa gave me a gorgeous diamond sun, the largest one I have ever seen. Mother gave me a diamond and sapphire necklace, one that she has worn a little while herself and therefore all the dearer to me, and from Uncle Corneil a most gorgeous stomacher of diamonds and one enormous pearl. They sent it to me last Sunday evening, and I was so excited about it that I made J take me up in a hansom to the house so that I could thank them myself. Then we went up to J's house to show it to his father and mother. And he got me there his present for me and showed it to me first in the hansom by the glare of a street lamp. It is the loveliest diamond collar, a tiara, or a pin. It is too dear of him to have given it to me; that and my engagement ring in one year are certainly enough to turn my head and quite spoil me."

Henry James in *The American Scene*, the illuminating account that he wrote of his return to his native land in 1905 after twenty years abroad, was struck by the seeming pointlessness of New York's display of wealth:

"The scene of our feast was a palace and the perfection of setting and service absolute; the ladies, beautiful, gracious and glittering with gems, were in tiaras and a semblance of court trains, a sort of predescribed official magnificence; but it was impossible not to ask oneself with what, in the wide American frame, such great matters might be supposed to consort or to rhyme. The material pitch was so high that it carried with it no social sequence, no application, and that, as a tribute to the ideal, to the exquisite, it wanted company, support, some sort of consecration."

James complains that after dinner there was nothing, as in London or Paris, to go "on" to; the guests could only scatter and go to bed. "A great court function would alone have properly crowned the hour." But what court function would there have been in republican Paris? And in London wasn't the court already considered by many as a bit of an anachronism, mainly useful as a symbol to hold a wide-flung empire together? And looking back at the other courts of Europe, turning the pages of coffee-table volumes filled with plates of dolled-up royalties waving from carriages or descending marble stairways, don't we see that the pageantry of monarchy, mostly on its last legs, no more "rhymed" or "consorted" with the general European frame of life than did James's New York dinner party with its American one? The Tiffany diamonds, after all, were just as beautiful worn by a Mrs. Vanderbilt or a Mrs. Gould as by an English princess or a Russian grand duchess. Maybe diamonds were forever, after all.

IF THE TIFFANYS COULD BE LIKENED TO THE MEDICI, LOUIS COMFORT TIFFANY MIGHT BE TO HIS FATHER, Charles, as Lorenzo il Magnifico was to Cosimo Pater Patriae. Charles was the great administrator, the solid, sober founder of the feast; Louis was the artist and art patron, the imaginative genius, but never a manager, never a conserver. When he died in 1932 he left only a fraction of the fortune bequeathed by his father three decades before. Yet if one owned today that same fraction of the objects Louis Tiffany designed and made in his lifetime, one would be rich indeed. The name Tiffany owes its fame equally to father and son.

Charles Tiffany understandably wanted his oldest son to go into the store, but he was a loving father, willing to support his children in any life work that they seriously elected, and he had soon to acknowledge that the boy who hated schoolwork and preferred to play with colored pebbles and bits of broken glass picked up on the beach during Montauk summers had better be allowed to skip college and study painting, so Louis went to Paris. He showed a true talent at an early age—his *Duane Street* anticipated the work of the Ashcan School by thirty years—but he nonetheless decided that his real gift was for design and decoration, and he gave up painting to form the Tiffany Studios, which, although independent of Tiffany & Co., used the store as an outlet for many of its products, particularly glassware. Louis also became an officer of the store, so his proud father could have him, after all, in the family business.

Tiffany Studios decorated many famous mansions and clubs, usually in exotic styles, Oriental or Byzantine or Moorish, or sometimes simply fantastic, but always exciting and luxurious, not quite Art Nouveau, but approaching it, as Robert Koch put it, in a blend of "Tiffany glass, Islamic carvings, embroidered hangings and painted friezes." Yet Tiffany's exoticism did not prevent him from giving the customer what the customer needed. A booklet published by a military organization praised the decorations of his Veterans' Room in the Seventh Regiment Armory, "the clamp and clang of iron, the metallic lustres, the ponderous beams" as "all clearly and undeniably assimilable and matchable with the huge, hard clanging ponderosities of wars and tramping regiments and armories."

But Louis Tiffany's greatest work was in glass. Early in his career he determined to find a way of incorporating brilliant colors and varied texture within the glass itself, bearing in mind Ruskin's warning: "No man who knows what painting means can endure a painted glass window which emulates a painter's work." In the opinion of the art critic Herwin Schaeffer, Tiffany's designs in stained glass were comparable

Floor Display, 1887

The second floor of the Union Square store displayed bronze and marble statuary as well as furnishings for the "tastefully" decorated Victorian home.

OVERLEAF
Tiffany Store at Union Square, 1870–1905

Tiffany & Co. was the first business establishment to open a store on Union Square, which, in 1870, was still in a residential neighborhood where many of Tiffany's affluent customers lived. The handsome façade of the five-story Tiffany building can be seen through the trees on the southwest corner of Sixteenth Street.

*Tiffany's London Store at 44
Old Bond Street (1932–WWII)*

Tiffany's
opened their first London
store in 1868 and eventually
relocated to this fashionable
shop at 44 Old Bond Street
in 1932.

LEFT
Tiffany House

The Charles
Tiffany house at Seventy-
second Street and Madison
Avenue was designed in 1885
by McKim, Mead and White.
Working with the architects,
Louis Comfort Tiffany
decorated the interior, which
he later occupied, in grand
Tiffany Art Nouveau style.

*Tiffany Store at Thirty-Seventh
Street and Fifth Avenue,
1905–1940*

Modeled by
McKim, Mead and White
after the sixteenth-century
Palazzo Grimani in Venice,
Tiffany's new store at Fifth
Avenue and Thirty-seventh
Street was hailed in 1905 "as
the highest mark of artistic
achievement of its time."

to the work of Post-Impressionist painters, because the soft transitions were eliminated and the areas of color set one against the other by black leading. Tiffany windows depicted brilliantly colored, highly realistic scenes and were in great demand for homes and churches. But the reaction was to come.

Up until the First World War, however, Louis Tiffany seemed to carry all before him, socially as well as professionally. Unlike his father, he lived on a splendid scale. Laurelton Hall, the summer mansion that he designed and built in Oyster Bay on Long Island, an asymmetrical edifice with a small stream running through the center of an enclosed court containing a clear glass fountain, was, in the words of Robert Koch, "an almost expressionist combination of simplified Art Nouveau forms with Islamic overtones, utterly unlike anything ever done before or since."

I have said that New York society was unleavened by artists. Tiffany changed all that. Sculptors, painters, musicians, and actors met the survivors and heirs of the old Four Hundred at his great costume ball in the winter of 1913, described by the New York *Times*, which should have known, having already covered the Vanderbilts' in 1883 and the Bradley Martins' in 1896, as "the most lavish costume fete ever seen in New York." It seemed an appropriate finale to the era that closed a year and a half later at Sarajevo. Even Tiffany's Dutch Renaissance mansion on Madison Avenue and Seventy-second Street, which covered ten thousand square feet and stood five tall stories high, was not large enough for the spectacle. The guests were invited by hieroglyphics on a roll of papyrus to come to the Tiffany Studios, where the central chamber had been transformed into a replica of ancient Alexandria, sumptuously decorated for the nuptials of Antony and Cleopatra, the representation of which, complete with Ethiopian slaves, gladiators, palanquins, and Roman soldiers, would constitute the main event of the evening. The guests were certainly cooperative; they submitted their costumes to the approval of a select committee, and the popular portraitist John Alexander, who went as a mummy, was even willing to remain propped up against a wall for much of the night.

Yet for all the elaboration of their efforts they look somewhat ridiculous in the photographs so profusely taken. I knew an old French lady, a survivor of the era, who coined a term for such goings-on: "silly-clever." She claimed that it covered much of the art and literature of the time. And indeed one wonders if there is not an aspect of the silly-clever in some of Louis Tiffany's art, beautiful though so much of it is, and if his severer critics did not seize upon this party as exemplifying what they felt to be meretricious in his glass. At any rate the ball seems to have coincided with the beginning of the downgrading of his work, a process that was not to be reversed until his death in 1932. Surely it would have come as a surprise to the art world in the years of the Great Depression had it been told of the magnificent display of Tiffany glass at the New-York Historical Society or of the prices now paid for his smallest pieces.

Charles Tiffany's sober way of living probably created better public relations for the salesman of luxury items than his son's flamboyant one. If you're in the business of selling jewelry and silverware, someone is always going to have it in for you—someone is always ready to moralize on the difference between the hard, soulless objects that you offer the public and his own bleeding heart. Kathleen Norris, the archsentimentalist of popular fiction, well illustrated this point in a short story for the *Ladies' Home Journal* in 1916. In it she portrays an out-of-town couple on a vacation to the wicked city, looking for the engagement ring that after some dozen years they are at last able to afford. They go, of course, to Tiffany's where, after much tremulous debate, the considerate wife selects a topaz, the one stone that seems within the range of her husband's budget. The narrator observes this of her:

"But when the salesman turned his back a moment she was not too absorbed to give a rapturous little squeeze to her husband's arm, and as their eyes met and the miracle of good and pure and fervent married love flashed in the look they exchanged, it seemed to me that I had at last found something worth buying in Tiffany's—the brightest jewel in the world!"

It may be worth pointing out that he had to go to Tiffany's to find it.

The real puritan will be even more suspicious of beautiful jewels and decorative objects than he will be of ugly and vulgar ones, for he will recognize their greater power to distract even a noble mind from spiritual matters. But that, of course, is only if spiritual matters are defined as having no relation whatever to material ones. To those of us, however, less mystical, who believe that a spiritual state can actually be approached through beautiful forms in the material world, loveliness even in an object as closely associated with pride and vanity as a diamond necklace may be elevating. And the policy of Charles Tiffany to maintain taste and proportion in every aspect of his store was the proper one to emphasize that his business was aimed at no less a goal than that of civilizing the community.

No exception was made even in the field of advertising, which, at least until David Ogilvy arrived in New York, was deemed practically synonymous with Yankee vulgarity. In the first century of its history Tiffany limited the information that it offered its public to the simplest statement of the nature of its business, printed on a large white square or oblong space, so that the reader might have imagined he was receiving a wedding announcement. Not until 1931, when the Depression had all but destroyed the luxury trades, was a silver beaker, like a crest, reluctantly added to the card. "Advertising's last stronghold of chaste austerity has now been breached," complained the *Engraving Bulletin*. "But even in capitulation one is still aware of a certain aloof quality."

Further discreet compromises were to follow. Tiffany products began to appear in photographs advertising haute couture and home interiors. The beautiful, elegant ladies of the 1930s, so firm of jaw, so poised, so arrogant, so vaguely defiant, the models for *Vogue* and *Harper's Bazaar*, now wore jewelry that a caption informed the reader were to be bought at Tiffany's. In time we were to see Tiffany tableware spread on a beach on which was sitting, her back to the camera, a totally nude young woman. But it always had to be a beautiful photograph.

Invitations engraved at Tiffany's were subject to similar restraints. Amy Vanderbilt, in two columns in the 1970s, had occasion to describe Tiffany's position with respect to wedding invitations. If the bride's parents were divorced, Tiffany's would allow the card to go out under their joint names "only after the customer had been advised it was not correct." A spokesman for the firm had suggested that the bid to the wedding go out under the mother's name and that for the reception (for which he was presumably paying) under the father's. The idea of a return card with a "Yes" or "No" was firmly vetoed as fitting only commercial invitations or charity events. It would be a slap in the face to friends who knew better. Nor was there any compromise with the format. Invitations had to be engraved in black on off-white or ecru paper.

Where time has completely borne out Tiffany's century-and-and-a-half-long war against tackiness is in the area of "free spirit" wedding bids. These in the late 1960s reached a peak of vulgarity, hotly defended by those who felt that forms were fetters and gush was truth. I think most of us twinge a bit today when we remember invitations that read: "On that day I will marry my friend, the one I laugh with, live for, dream with, love," or that had quotations from Kahlil Gibran or photographs of sunrises, or worse yet, the humorous kind, with a cartoon of kids playing dress-up in wedding clothes. One even heard of a card where the bride and groom were depicted in swimsuits, he with a tall silk hat, she with a veil, crouched at the edge of a pool

Lady Pearson's Bicycle

This Tiffany silver bicycle, with hand-chased decoration, was presented to Lady Pearson by her husband, Sir Weetman Pearson, on a visit to New York in 1894.

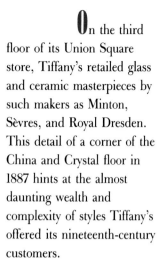

Floor Display, 1887

On the third floor of its Union Square store, Tiffany's retailed glass and ceramic masterpieces by such makers as Minton, Sèvres, and Royal Dresden. This detail of a corner of the China and Crystal floor in 1887 hints at the almost daunting wealth and complexity of styles Tiffany's offered its nineteenth-century customers.

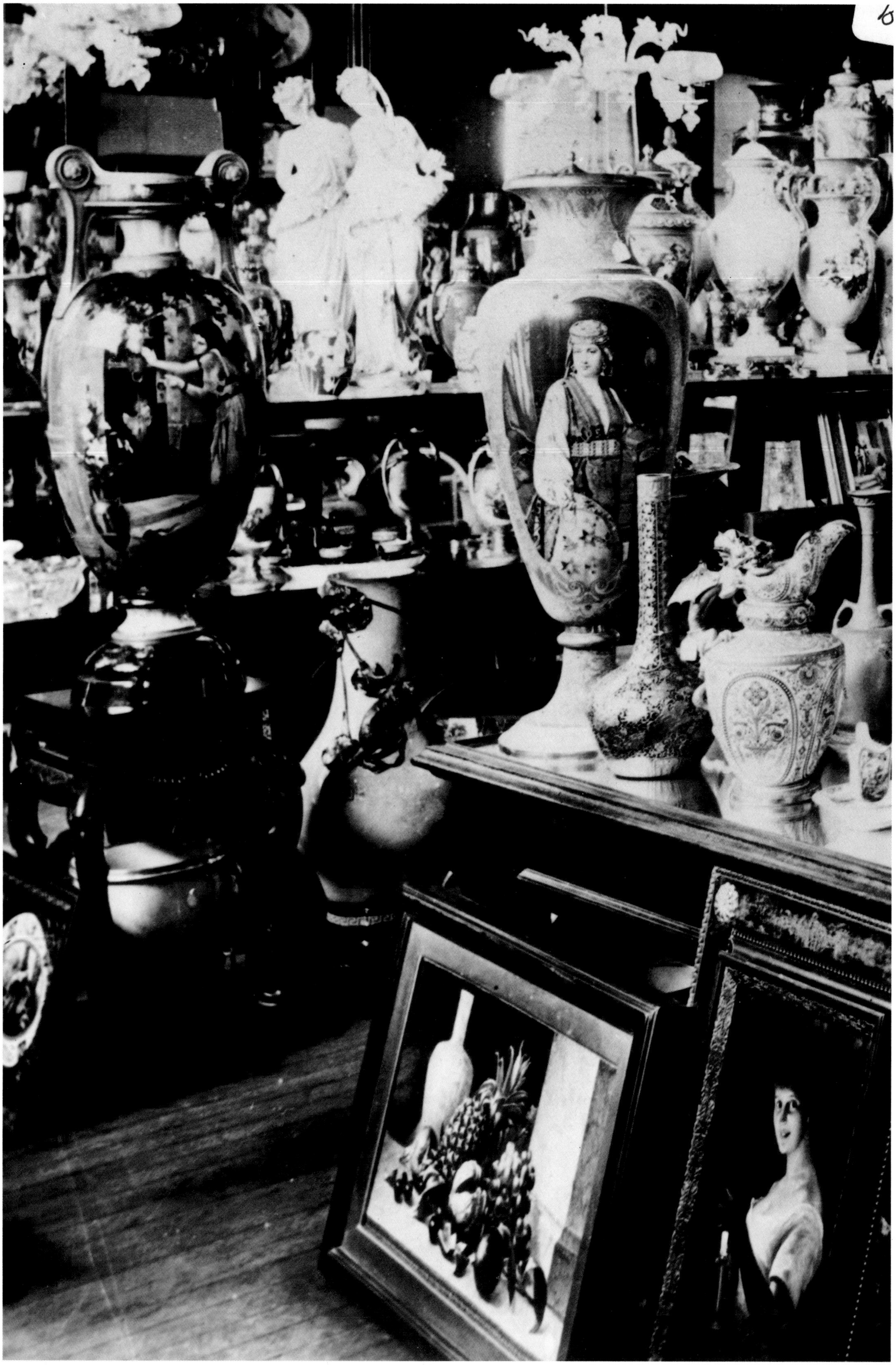

The Punch Bowl from the
Battleship New Jersey, 1906

The Indianapolis Race Cup,
First Awarded in 1909

On August 14,
1907, the state of New Jersey
presented a fifty-seven-piece
Tiffany silver service to the
battleship named in its
honor. The punch bowl,
decorated with naval motifs as
well as the personifications of
Liberty and Prosperity,
traveled with the ship during
World War I. During battle it
was struck with a piece of
shrapnel. The officers who
commanded the ship refused
to have it repaired.

*Height: 21 inches (53.3 cm); length of
base: 32 inches (81.3 cm)*
*United States Navy Collection,
photograph courtesy of the New Jersey
State Museum*

Commissioned
in 1909 by the Wheeler and
Schebler Company of
Indianapolis, makers of
carburetors, this sterling silver
racing trophy was awarded
annually to the driver of the
Indianapolis 500 who led the
race at the 400-mile marker.
After car owner Harry Hartz
(seen in photograph) won the
trophy three consecutive times
in the 1930s, the trophy was
retired.

*Indianapolis Motor Speedway Hall of
Fame Museum*

over the legend: "We're about to take the plunge." If Tiffany's hadn't existed, it would have had to be invented.

Perhaps the greatest row between the store and its critics occurred over one of Gene Moore's famous window displays in 1983. Designed by Robert Keane McKinley, it showed a scene of garbage bags, crumpled beer cans, a graffiti-covered wood fence, a sign that read "No Loitering," and two human figures, one standing and one sitting on the ground. Standing was a bum, holding a bottle of J&B Scotch, and seated, her legs askew, between two plastic containers which presumably held all her worldly goods, was a bag lady, reading a copy of *House & Garden*. And snaking across the foreground was a necklace with twenty-seven carats of diamonds.

The outcry was loud. Columnists and commentators were vociferous on the subject of Tiffany's heartlessness and bad taste, and the window display was withdrawn, although stoutly defended by both the artist and Moore. I quite agree with them. There can be nothing offensive in an art that juxtaposes the wretched and sordid with the opulent and magnificent. The artist was making a statement about our city and in my opinion an entirely valid one. It is subject to different and interesting interpretations, and I do not offer one. I simply point out that T. S. Eliot loved to contrast the glory of urban pasts with the wasteland of urban presents.

THE SECOND WORLD WAR BROUGHT TIFFANY & CO. ONLY A BRIEF RECOVERY FROM THE RAVAGES OF THE Depression years, and by the mid-1950s a too-conservative philosophy of merchandising, out of keeping with the times, had finally induced the stockholders to look for new management. The era of Walter Hoving began. What the staff called "the great white elephant sale" of all the wares the new chairman disliked, including silver plate and leather handbags, was held; the store was completely redecorated; the former president of the Parsons School of Design, Van Day Truex, was retained to take charge of design for china and silver, and the great French jewelry designer Jean Schlumberger for jewelry. "Aesthetics, if properly understood," Hoving maintained, "will almost always increase sales." He was right. The store recovered and prospered.

Nothing would induce Hoving to cater to the popular taste if that taste was bad. Buyers who wanted diamond rings for men could go elsewhere. It was the same with items, not necessarily in bad taste, but common and easily obtainable. People didn't come from St. Louis or Chicago to buy what they could get in a drugstore at home. "What you find at Tiffany's can't be bought anywhere else." If a customer protested that he should be provided with what he reasonably desired, Hoving would retort: "What you want is your business. What we sell is ours." And he sounded the grim warning that Loeser's, McCreery's, and Wanamaker's, three great stores, had all gone out of business in New York after they started to trade down.

When John F. Kennedy approached Tiffany's to design special calendar plaques as gifts for White House staffers to mark the days of the Cuban missiles crisis, he wanted them made of Lucite. Hoving refused, insisting on sterling silver, and Kennedy went elsewhere, but when he saw what he ultimately got, he returned to Tiffany's. And when Dwight D. Eisenhower, purchasing a gold medallion for Mamie, asked, smiling, if the President of the United States did not get a discount at Tiffany's, he was told that Abraham Lincoln had not received one.

Yet Hoving did not brush off the T-shirt-and-blue-jeans set. "The richest kids wear the worst clothes," he pointed out. It was better to get them into the shop and then see what could be done for them. He changed the image of the store from one that catered only to the very rich to one that offered anyone interested the best for the least. Something might be expensive at Tiffany's, but you couldn't get it cheaper anywhere else.

The very rich, however, were by no means neglected. The new society in New York was very different from what had been found in the pages of the old Social Register. It was a society, to use its own favorite term, of "doers"; the women were as busy as the men. Old money mixed with new; investment bankers with cosmeticians; corporation lawyers with artists and TV commentators; bishops with real estate operators. Even the underworld, alas, was at times visible. But it was also a society that cared even more than had its predecessors about looks, about keeping slim and trim, about dress and decor and jewelry. Never, except perhaps in eighteenth-century France, had the upper rungs of the social ladder been more brightly burnished. And as the jet kept this world in constant touch with its counterparts all over the globe, a certain uniformity in good taste and splendor began to appear in large houses and apartments from Rome to Hong Kong. One has only to turn the pages of *House & Garden* or *Town & Country* or *Architectural Digest* to see this abundantly illustrated.

Tiffany's took on a major role in this development of international good taste. It had long had stores in London and Paris, but now it opened branches in Boston, Chicago, San Francisco, Beverly Hills, Dallas, Houston, and Atlanta. As affluence spread, people who had never dreamed that they would be able to entertain as did the hostesses they read about in the social columns began to wonder if they couldn't. Tiffany's instituted a spring show of table settings in which such New York ladies as Mrs. Vincent Astor, Kitty Carlisle, Diana Vreeland, and Mrs. Albert Lasker set up their own tables, using their own linen and antique accessories. As one observer put it: "Mrs. Queens and Mrs. Brooklyn hurried to the store to see how Mrs. Manhattan did it."

Mrs. William Paley's table setting, called "Breakfast at Tiffany's," was in part designed by her friend the author Truman Capote. Capote's heroine Holly Golightly expressed some of the affectionate feeling that the store evoked in its public now that it had become, in its long history, almost synonymous with the style and elegance of the city. When Holly got the blues she would hop into a taxi and go to Tiffany's. "It calms me down right away, the quietness and the proud look of it: nothing very bad could happen to you there, not with those kind men in their nice suits and the lovely smell of silver and alligator wallets."

Letitia Baldrige, Tiffany's former director of public relations, recalls that when Audrey Hepburn and George Peppard, in a three-minute scene from the movie *Breakfast at Tiffany's,* based on Capote's novel, had to be filmed walking through the ground floor of the store to make a purchase, Hoving insisted for security reasons that Tiffany's salespeople play themselves. The film company had to pay each of them overtime as well as the regular extra's fee and a stiff bill for the additional insurance necessary because the jewelry had not been placed in the vault after closing time. But it was a great thing for Tiffany's public relations. The film and television reruns were seen by millions, and for years afterward tourists would come into the store to ask for the restaurant.

The store caught the passing glance of another famous novelist of Gotham ways and manners. Anita Loos, speaking at her eightieth birthday party, quoted from *Gentlemen Prefer Blondes:*

"So Mr. Eisman gave me quite a nice string of pearls, and he gave Dorothy a diamond pin, and we all went to the Colony for dinner, and we all went to a show and supper at the Trocadero, and we all spent quite a pleasant evening."

Where, she went on ruefully to ask, in our day of soaring prices, would a man get his hands on the kind of money needed to give a girl "quite a pleasant evening"? "What would Mr. Eisman give her today? He'd give her some subway tokens. That's why Tiffany's sells special silver token containers."

In 1850 Tiffany's opened its first Paris store at 79 rue Richelieu. By 1910 Tiffany's had relocated on the more fashionable Place de l'Opéra and boasted this interior inspired by the Hall of Mirrors at Versailles.

*Charles L. Tiffany and
Charles T. Cook*

Charles L. Tiffany is seen here in his Union Square store at the age of eighty-seven, with Charles T. Cook, who assumed the reins of leadership after Tiffany died in 1902.

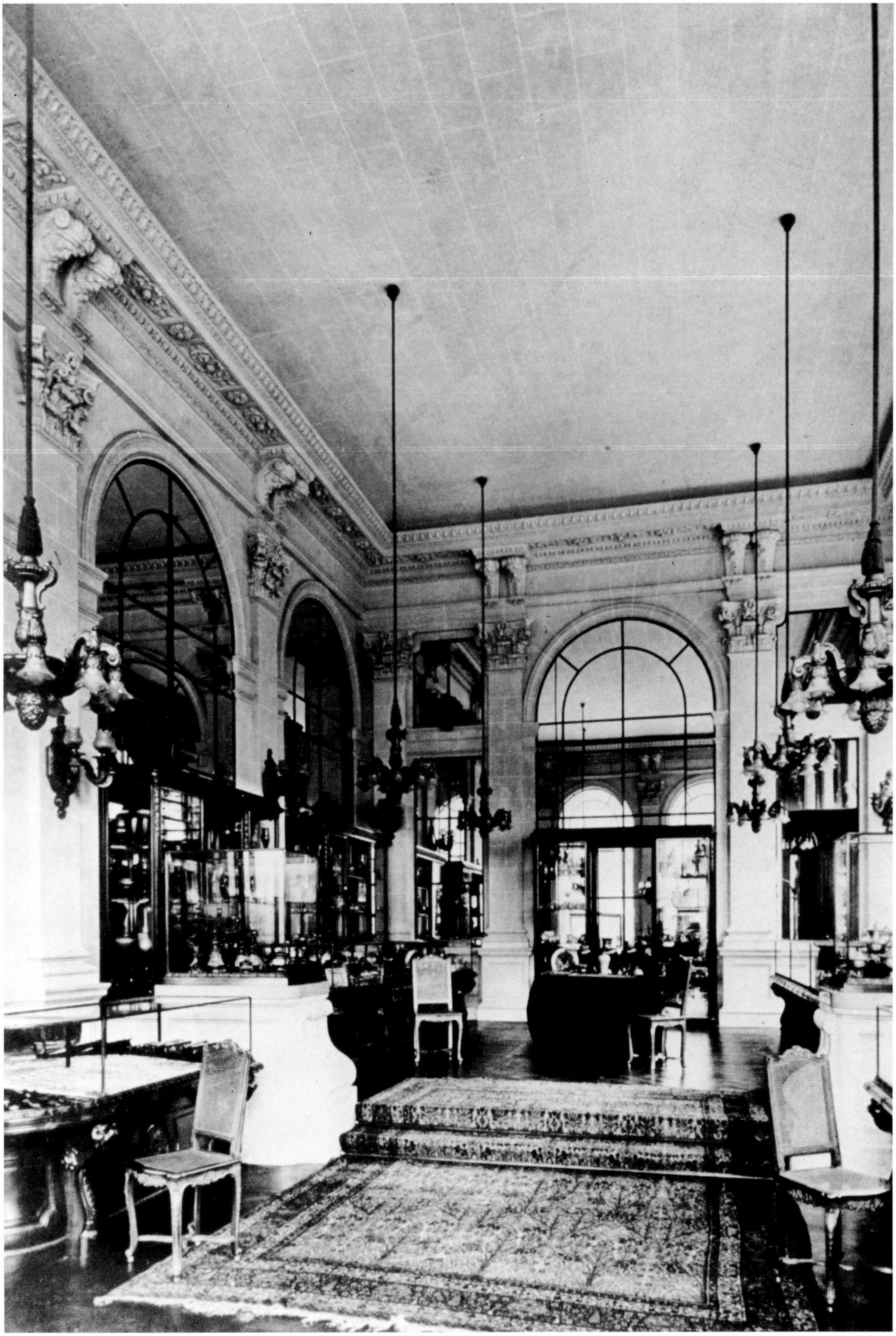

HARRY PLATT, A GREAT-GRANDSON OF LOUIS TIFFANY, WHO WAS PRESIDENT OF THE STORE UNDER THE Hoving chairmanship and in particular charge of jewelry, acted as a kind of global ambassador from the firm to the world capitals of fashion and taste. He even established a Tiffany's in Mitsukoshi, the giant Tokyo department store, to sell jewelry to the now emancipated Japanese women who in the past had not been considered of enough social importance by their consorts to merit the expense. And for two decades he gave a semiannual December ball at the Versailles Room of the St. Regis in which he quite deliberately selected as his guests the most beautiful as well as the best-dressed ladies in society. The event became a kind of ritual celebration of international beauty and style, heavily covered by the press. But because the subjects photographed were dressed in what most strikingly became them, what they most easily and naturally wore, there was none of the "silly-clever" aspect attached to the snapshots as at Platt's great-grandfather's ball in 1913. The jewels as well as the dresses belonged to the epoch, and even if a subsequent age should frown at its worldliness—as it probably will—I doubt it will find fault with its taste.

I remember, many years ago, going through the albums of the Jekyll Island Club, that onetime favorite Georgian resort of New York bankers and their Wall Street counsel, shortly before its demolition in favor of a housing development, and being struck by the corpulence of so many of its members, both male and female. On the golf course, on the croquet lawn, or simply relaxing in rocking chairs on a broad piazza, there was something faintly absurd about them, a kind of perspiring puffiness, the abandonment of any kind of hope that anything was ever going to fit. And didn't their avoirdupois make their worldliness seem more worldly? I was reminded of John Armstrong Chanler's cruel sonnet about the diamond horseshoe at the opera, and of radical cartoons that show the rich as bloated. Perhaps it smacks of arrogance to take so little care of one's appearance. There may even be a kind of democracy in the effort made today by the commercially successful to look well to the public that buys their product. I turn in relief from the Jekyll Island Club album to the pictures of Harry's parties.

The growing affluence of America has made Tiffany products available to a much larger segment of the population than formerly, and John Loring, who succeeded Truex as director of design and brought in Paloma Picasso, has taken full advantage of this. Because of the very speed with which some young persons have become prosperous today, they do not have to go through the period of clutter and curlicues so favored by the newly rich of the nineteenth century. The yuppie of the 1980s has a clearer and less prejudiced eye than his counterpart (if counterpart he really had) of seventy years ago.

"Van Truex," Loring recalls, "could hold up a white Wedgwood plate and say, 'This is perfection.' But he might say that same thing about a wonderfully gaudy Imari plate. With Van spending less and less time at the store, there was a danger of that second side being forgotten. There was a sense of things fading into beige blandness. I think that's why I was brought in."

Loring was brought in by Walter Hoving. He guided Tiffany's design and image through its five years of Avon ownership that followed Hoving's retirement and on into Tiffany's new era of independence following the company's leveraged buy-out masterminded by Tiffany's new chairman, William Chaney. Loring continues to play the role of tastemaker today, and to an audience ready to learn. But he knows that the standards can never be allowed to slip. That is the Tiffany trademark.

Nobody has better described the loving care and labor that goes into the consummate craftmanship of the Tiffany artisans than Letitia Baldrige:

"To watch silver designer Oscar Riedener was to watch patience, as he pondered and tested for one entire week the shape of a knife blade on a new silver flatware pattern before making his decision. To watch Arthur Gough was to watch patience as he sat in the calligraphy department, spending three months buried like a medieval monk in his tower; however, instead of illuminating the Bible, he was working on a few letters of his new alphabet of script, which would be immediately copied and used by the country's leading stationers, engravers and printers. To watch the head of the engraving department, Bill Demarest, was to watch patience as he presided over each order with the same meticulous paternal pride, whether it was the engraving of two initials on a baby spoon ordered by Mary Smith, or the Pope's coat of arms on a letter box ordered by the President of the United States."

Louis Auchincloss

Tiffany Jewelry Design Studio

Drawing for a "special order" gold and diamond necklace being drawn by Mr. Maurice Galli, senior jewelry designer, 1986.

1837–1869

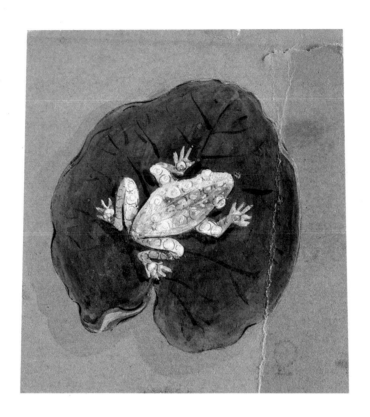

On September 21, 1837, two enterprising young New Englanders, Charles L. Tiffany and John P. Young, opened a "Stationery and Dry Goods" shop at 259 Broadway in a simple wood-and-brick structure opposite New York's magnificent neoclassical city hall. They had invested a modest one thousand dollars borrowed from Tiffany's father in their business, whose opening day receipt fell a few cents short of five dollars.

However humble its first sale, the firm of Tiffany & Young prospered as New Yorkers vied for the rare and often exotic goods the discerning eye of Mr. Tiffany discovered in the great American importing centers of New York and Boston.

In 1841 Tiffany & Young took in a third partner, John L. Ellis, and the more soundly capitalized firm of Tiffany, Young and Ellis was soon able to add important stocks of English silver along with Continental crystal, porcelain, and personal accessories unavailable in other New York stores.

Gold jewelry was introduced in 1845 and Swiss watches, bronze statuary, and jewelry set with precious stones in 1847. By 1848 a new Tiffany goldsmithing shop was producing the first Tiffany-made jewelry; that same year John Young, on a trip to Paris, was able to purchase the jewels of Maria Amelia, wife of the recently deposed French King, Louise Philippe.

The New York press dubbed Tiffany "King of Diamonds" when he put the French crown jewels on display, and from that day forward, Tiffany's took its place as the greatest of America's jewelers.

Tiffany's successes allowed him in 1851 to bring New York's leading silver manufacturer, John C. Moore, into the firm, assuring its future world leadership in the silver industry.

In thirty years the firm grew from a modest boutique to a great emporium. At the Paris Exposition Universelle of 1867 they won the first medal ever to be awarded to an American silver maker.

This first period saw the origin of the famous "Tiffany blue" packaging (the most fashionable decorating color of the period) and its logo derived from the gilded wooden letters used on the firm's storefront.

OPPOSITE PAGE
Cyrus Field Transatlantic Cable Section, Letter, and Gold Box, 1858

This elaborately engraved gold box was presented to Cyrus W. Field by the City of New York to commemorate "his skill, fortitude and perseverance, in originating and completing the first enterprise for an ocean telegraph successfully accomplished on 5th August 1858." Charles Tiffany capitalized on the event, buying up twenty miles of extra cable (some retrieved from the ocean floor) and selling the souvenirs with an accompanying letter of authenticity, signed by Field.

The Metropolitan Museum of Art, gift of Cyrus W. Field, 1892

BELOW
Tiffany Design Department Drawing for the Congressional Medal of Honor

OVERLEAF
Astor Tea Set

The Rococo Revival tea and coffee service was given as a wedding gift to Caroline Astor, the undisputed queen of New York society during the last quarter of the nineteenth century. Together with her social arbiter, Ward McAllister, Mrs. Astor formulated the famed Four Hundred, a social roster of New York's most fashionable society. (Only four hundred guests could fit comfortably into Mrs. Astor's ballroom.)

Tea and Coffee Service: Collection of Mr. and Mrs. R. Thornton Wilson

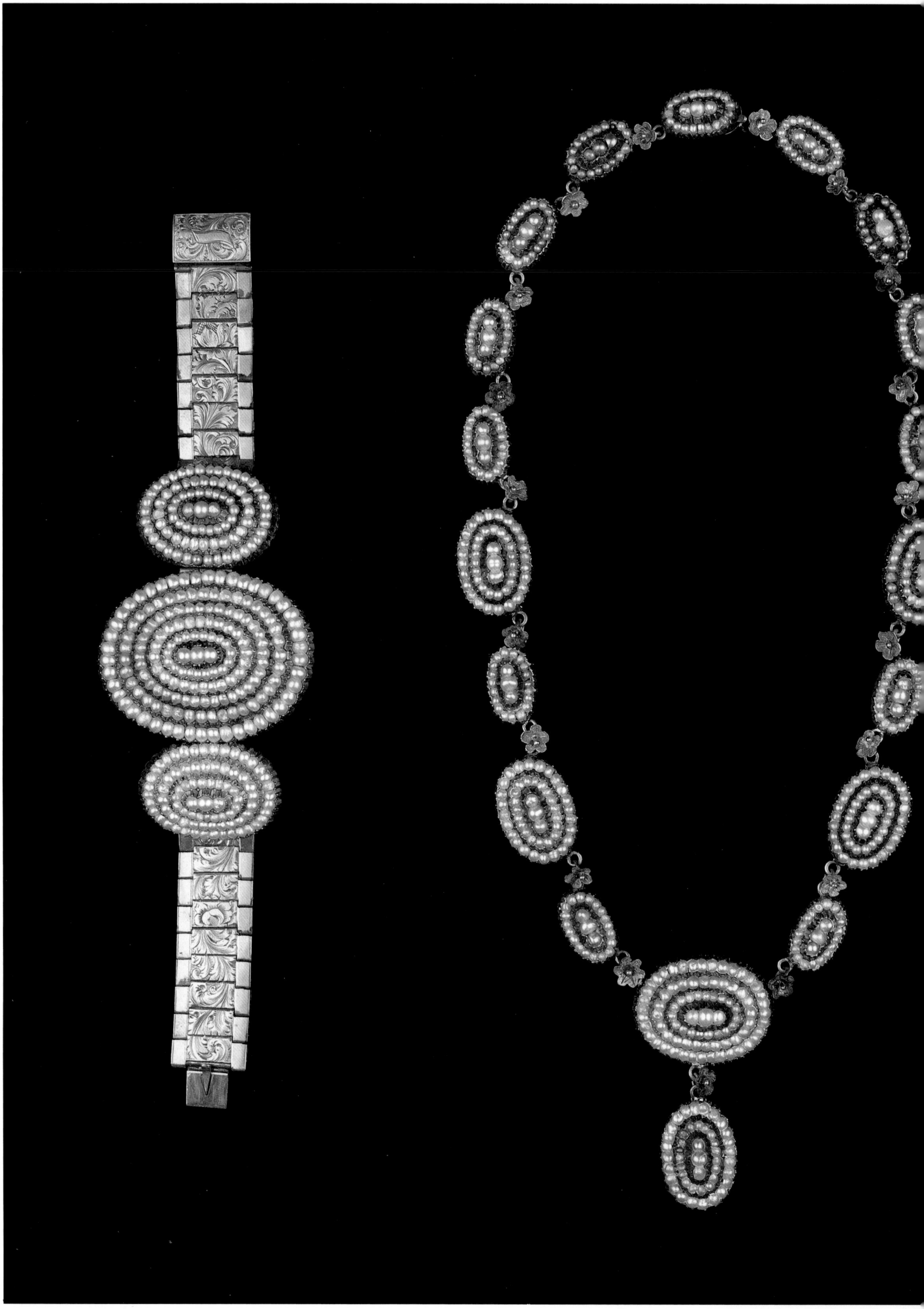

*Mathew Brady Portrait of
Mary Todd Lincoln Wearing
Pearls, 1861*

OVERLEAF
*Tom Thumb Horse and
Carriage*

Abraham
Lincoln's First Lady was
poorly received by
Washington society. She
consoled herself with
extravagant spending sprees.
In this Inauguration
photograph of 1861, she wears
a seed-pearl parure purchased
by President Lincoln from
Tiffany's 550 Broadway store
for $530.

New-York Historical Society

LEFT
*Mrs. Lincoln's Pearl Necklace
and Bracelets Purchased by
Abraham Lincoln from
Tiffany's in 1861*

Rare Book and Special Collections
Division of the Library of Congress,
Washington, D.C.

P.T. Barnum's
American Museum was
located on Broadway just six
blocks from Tiffany's.
Specializing in the eccentric,
Barnum featured the midgets
Tom Thumb and Lavinia
Warren in his shows both at
home and abroad. Staging
their wedding at the socially
fashionable Grace Episcopal
Church in New York, he
created such a sensation that
the streets were jammed with
onlookers desiring to catch a
glimpse of the "little people."
For their wedding, Tiffany &
Co. presented the couple with
a silver-filigree horse and
carriage studded with garnets
and rubies.

*Middleborough Historical Museum,
Middleboro, Massachusetts*

TIFFANY'S
150 YEARS

51

PRECEDING OVERLEAF
Civil War Sword, 1864

*Detail of Hilt and Scabbard of
Sword, 1864*

With the
outbreak of the Civil War,
Charles Tiffany, like many
other New York retailers,
began selling military
paraphernalia to the Union
Army. Among these items
were six hundred presentation
swords to be awarded in
recognition of heroic acts.
These swords show stylistic
similarities to swords of
Nicholas Noel Boutet, the
famous Versailles gunsmith of
the Napoleonic period.
Original orders to Tiffany &
Co. for Civil War arms are
shown here with General
John Wynn Davidson's sword.

The illustrated
Civil War sword was designed
and made by Tiffany's and
presented in 1864 to General
John Wynn Davidson, the
"Hero of Bayou Meto and
Little Rock," by the privates
and noncommissioned officers
of the First Iowa Veteran
Calvary. On the hilt, the
figure of Liberty stands
beneath the American eagle.
General Davidson's
monogram ornaments the
scabbard.

1870–1899

In the last thirty years of the nineteenth century, Tiffany & Co. outfitted America for the Gilded Age, that continuous celebration of its newfound prosperity. The great American families flocked to Tiffany's to order their jewels, the invitations to their social events, their private silver patterns, and their commemorative objects.

John C. Moore's designer son, Edward C. Moore, expressed the period's fascination with Japan's opening to the outside world with his remarkable Japanese Revival style silver.

This was the period of Tiffany's masterpieces: the Bryant Cup, the Adams Vase, and the Magnolia Vase. Tiffany's garnered prizes wherever its goods were exhibited.

In this period, too, the most acclaimed American gemologist, George F. Kunz, joined Tiffany's. He began work at age twenty-one in 1877, the year the Tiffany Diamond was purchased. By 1889 he had assembled the finest collection of American gemstones, which Tiffany's exhibited at the Paris Exposition of 1889 and which J. Pierpoint Morgan later purchased for the New York Museum of Natural History.

Some fifty years after its founding, Tiffany's owned thriving branch stores on London's Old Bond Street and Paris's Place de l'Opéra and held appointments as gold- and silversmith to every crowned head in Europe.

Charles Tiffany had become a true prince of commerce and his store had become an American institution whose name stood for quality throughout the world.

Tiffany's Bryant Vase, a masterpiece of high-style Victorian design, combines unparalleled workmanship with symbolic tribute to the famous American poet William Cullen Bryant. The lower portion of the body and handles are decorated with American cornstalks, while bobolinks perched among the handles' cornstalks refer to Bryant's humorous poem "Robert O' Lincoln," which extols the carefree and apolitical life of the humble bobolink, who presumably sided neither with Robert E. Lee nor with Abraham Lincoln.

Bryant admiringly described the vase as "the work of artists who are the worthy successors of Benvenuto Cellini. . . ."

LEFT
The Bryant Vase, 1875–76

In honor of William Cullen Bryant's eightieth birthday, a group of friends presented the great poet/journalist with a massive silver vase in the shape of a Greek amphora ornamented with, among other things, American corn. Designed by James H. Whitehouse, the Bryant Vase was exhibited at the 1876 Centennial Exhibition in Philadelphia. It was described by the Philadelphia *Times* as one of "the most wonderful specimens of pure repoussé chasing in the Exhibition . . ."

Height: 33⅜ inches (84.8 cm)
The Metropolitan Museum of Art, gift of William Cullen Bryant, 1877

Found in the Kimberley mines of South Africa in 1877 and purchased by Charles Tiffany that same year for eighteen thousand dollars, the Tiffany Diamond is the largest and finest canary diamond in the world. Weighing 128.51 carats, it has an unusual ninety facets that make the celebrated gem appear to smolder as if lit by an inner flame.

"**M**an is the only animal that blushes, or needs to," wrote Mark Twain. Riverboat pilot, newspaper reporter, and humorist, Twain was aptly described as "the Lincoln of our literature," by William D. Howells, editor of the *Atlantic Monthly*. Twain's wife, Olivia, was a loyal patron of Tiffany's, and Twain commissioned Louis Comfort Tiffany's decorating firm, Associated Artists, to stencil gold and silver motifs on the walls and ceilings of several rooms of his Hartford, Connecticut, mansion.

Pictured here are a baptismal bowl, baby cup and plate, and flat silver once owned by members of the family, as well as first editions of Twain's early books *A Tramp Abroad* and *The Innocents Abroad*.

When Marie Louise Mackay asked her husband, "Can I have enough silver from our own mine to make . . . a dinner service . . . made by the finest silversmith in the country?" her husband, "Silver Bonanza King" John Mackay, complied. Designed under the direction of Edward C. Moore in 1877, the "Dinner and Dessert Service for Twenty-four Persons" was fashioned from 14,719 ounces of silver which Mackay had shipped from the Comstock Lode. The service reportedly took two hundred men two years to complete and was shown by Tiffany & Co. at the Paris Exposition of 1878 where Tiffany's exhibit was awarded the grand prize for silverware.

Discontented with New York society, Mrs. Mackay moved to Europe and used her service regularly to entertain royalty and dignitaries.

The Tête-à-Tête Set from the Mackay Silver Service, 1878

The "Silver Bonanza King" Mackay's tête-à-tête set's elaborate floral chasings incorporate the Irish shamrock and Scottish thistle, symbols of Mrs. Mackay's ancestry. The set was much admired when it was exhibited in the 1878 Paris Exposition, and one critic accurately described it as "graceful and shapely and gorgeous in workmanship."

Selection of Silver in Japanesque Style, Late 1870s

Tiffany's Japanese Revival silver with its applied fish, flowers, and insects in gold, copper, or silver are among the most remarkable achievements of the Aesthetic Movement in America. Designed under the direction of Edward C. Moore, and introduced by Tiffany's at the Union Square store in 1876, "Japanesque" silverwares were an immediate success, first in America and then two years later abroad when they were shown to universal acclaim at the Paris Exposition of 1878.

PITCHER: The Virginia Carroll Crawford Collection, courtesy of the High Museum of Art, Atlanta, Georgia

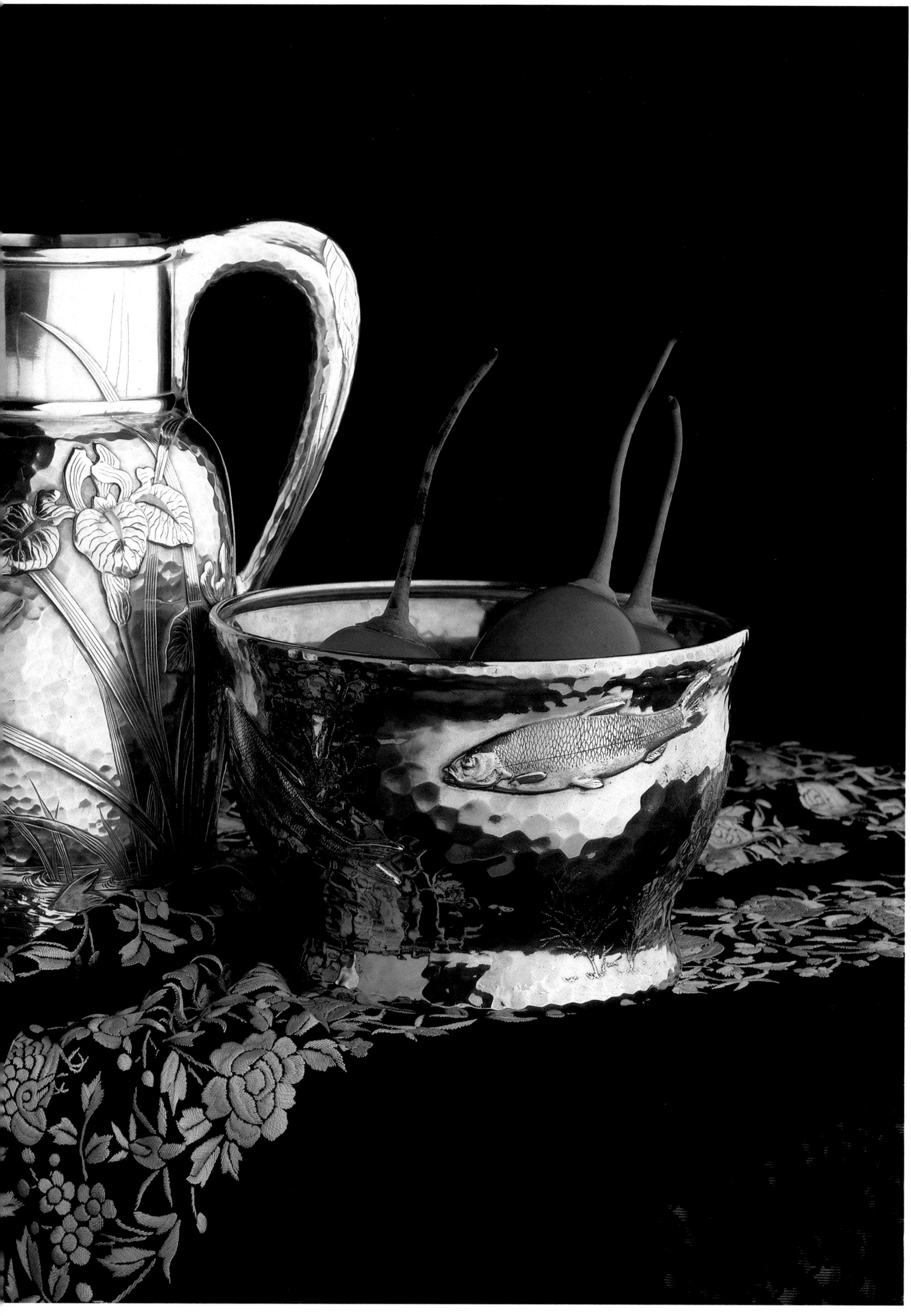

House of Cards

esigned by C.
C. Carryl for Tiffany & Co.
in 1879, these so-called
"transformation" cards, in
which the suit symbols were
wittily incorporated into the
card's overall pictorial
decoration, were all the rage
at fashionable euchre and
whist parties in the second
half of the nineteenth
century.

*The Preservation Society of Newport
County, the Elms, Newport, Rhode
Island*

*Japanese Vase, Creamer, and
Sugar Bowl*

The
asymmetrical and often
esoteric arrangement of
patterns found in Japanese
design became the
distinguishing feature of
Tiffany's finest silverwares of
the 1870s. The applied fish
decoration and lily pads on
the illustrated vase, creamer,
and sugar bowl are typical of
the fanciful American
ornamental style of the 1870s
so influenced by Japanese
prints.

VASE: The Metropolitan Museum of
Art, purchase, Mr. and Mrs. H. O.
H. Frelinghuysen Gift, 1982

CREAMER AND SUGAR BOWL: The
Metropolitan Museum of Art,
purchase, the Edgar J. Kaufmann
Foundation Gift, 1969

PAGE 68
*Audubon Flatware and Tea Set
Designed by Edward C. Moore*

Although
Admiral Perry opened Japan
to the West in 1854, it was
not until 1867 at the Paris
Exposition Universelle that
Japanese art had an impact
on American design. The
large Japanese exhibit at the
Paris Fair intrigued Edward
C. Moore, chief designer for
Tiffany's, who was then
overseeing the Tiffany
exhibit. The illustrated tea
kettle, sugar bowl, and
creamer with the chased
decoration of birds and
flowers is a precursor to
"Audubon" flatware, designed
and patented by Moore in
1871.

PAGE 69
*Liqueur Set, Japanesque Style,
1878*

In the 1870s,
Japanism and the Aesthetic
Movement became almost
synonymous. Every stylish
house included a "Japanese"
corner in its interior
decoration based on what
were believed to be Japanese
principles. The "Japanese"
shapes of Tiffany silver of the
period were derived from
vegetable forms, such as the
gourd shape of this Tiffany
Japanese Revival style tray,
whose applied copper and
silver decorations repeat the
gourd theme.

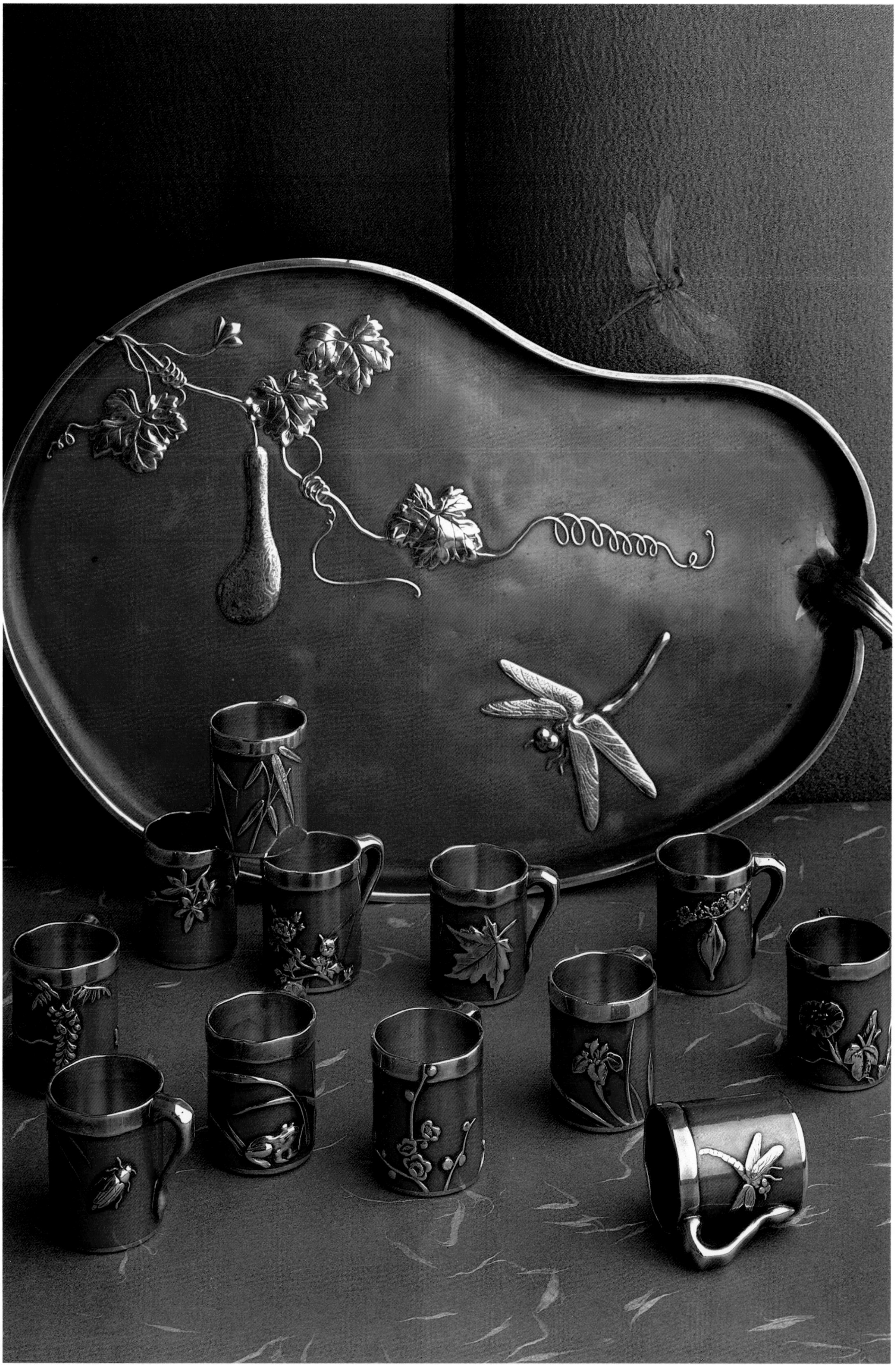

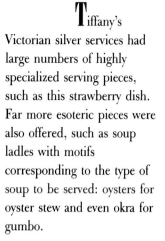

Silver Strawberry Dish, c. 1890

Tiffany's Victorian silver services had large numbers of highly specialized serving pieces, such as this strawberry dish. Far more esoteric pieces were also offered, such as soup ladles with motifs corresponding to the type of soup to be served: oysters for oyster stew and even okra for gumbo.

BOTTOM LEFT
"Sarasenic" Tea Set

This outstanding tea set was designed by Edward C. Moore, Tiffany's great nineteenth-century designer and the foremost American silversmith of his day. The enameled, etched, and gilded decoration displays Islamic and Indian influences. As one of the leading designers who disseminated the taste for Orientalia in the United States, Moore formed a superb private collection of Eastern and Near Eastern artifacts, which in turn inspired Louis Comfort Tiffany.

The Metropolitan Museum of Art, gift of a Friend of the Museum, 1897

Vanderbilt Christening Set

Children's table sets were already popular gifts in America by the mid-1800s. This set, with applied die-rolled decoration, was given to her grandson by Mary Louise Kissam Vanderbilt, wife of railroad magnate William Henry Vanderbilt, whose astute business transactions did so much to bolster the family fortune amassed by his father "Commodore" Cornelius Vanderbilt.

The Vanderbilt Dessert Service

Mrs. William K. ("Alva") Vanderbilt was one of the only New York socialites to offer real competition to Caroline Astor, the undisputed leader of New York society. In 1883 Mrs. Vanderbilt pointedly neglected to invite Mrs. Astor to a lavish costume ball to be held in the Vanderbilt's Fifth Avenue mansion, explaining that "The Vanderbilts do not know the Astors." Swallowing her pride, Mrs. Astor commented, "I think the Vanderbilts' time has come," and hastily sent her calling card. An invitation was forthcoming.

The illustrated dessert set is the Vanderbilts' exclusive Tiffany flatware pattern designed by Charles T. Grosjean and delivered in 1885.

OPPOSITE PAGE

*Silver and Ivory Cigar Holder,
1881*

This silver and
ivory cigar holder made by
Tiffany's in 1881 clearly
exhibits the whirling reversed
curve forms and flowers of
Japanese Revival design that
were already suggestive of Art
Nouveau, or the "Tiffany
style."

Tiffany Flasks from the 1880s

Hunting's great
popularity during the second
half of the nineteenth century
spurred an avid interest in
flasks richly decorated with
etched hunting scenes,
dancing nymphs, grinning
satyrs, and other assorted
delights.

PAGE 74

*Original Drawings for
Nineteenth-Century Tiffany
Catalogues and Calendars*

The
imagination, charm, and vigor
of these Tiffany graphic
designs typify the exemplary
level of invention and
craftsmanship that has kept
Tiffany & Co. a leader in
design throughout its one
hundred and fifty years.

The "North Wind" and
lilac motifs for winter and
spring 1885, as well as the

unfinished floriate design for
summer 1883, are
masterpieces of nineteenth-
century graphic invention.

The "Tiffany blue" used
on the second cover from the
top has remained a symbol of
Tiffany's. It was the most
popular color in decoration at
the time the company was
founded in 1837, and was
then to be found everywhere
in Louis-Philippe and
William IV design.

Invitation to the Statue of Liberty Inauguration

President Grover Cleveland accepted the invitation to attend the celebrations for the Statue of Liberty just in time to have his name included on the official invitation. Tiffany designed and engraved the invitations for the opening celebration of Miss Liberty on October 28, 1886.

The Bartholdi Testimonial

The *World* newspaper, under the leadership of Joseph Pulitzer, raised enough funds to present Frédéric Auguste Bartholdi, sculptor of the Statue of Liberty, with the Bartholdi Testimonial on November 13, 1886. Designed by James Whitehouse (known also for designing the "Great Seal" on the reverse side of the one-dollar bill), the impressively scaled testimonial rests on a polished block of petrified wood. Its silver globe is surmounted by a replica of Liberty's hand holding the torch.

Its inscription reads: "A Tribute from the New York *World* and Over 121,000 Americans to Auguste Bartholdi and the Great Liberty-Loving People of France."

From The World, *November 13, 1886*
Height: 38 inches (96.50 cm)
Musée Bartholdi, Colmar, France

Searles Flatware

Known as the "Searles Service," this silver-gilt dessert service, designed by Charles T. Grosjean, was made in 1886 for Mary Frances Hopkins, reputedly the wealthiest widow in America.

In 1887, surprising both family and friends, she married Edward T. Searles, a handsome interior decorator over twenty years her junior. Her will later created a much publicized sensation: to the dismay of her family, Mary Frances left her entire multimillion-dollar fortune to Searles.

OPPOSITE PAGE
Indian Handle Flatware

Charles Grosjean, who designed much of Tiffany's flatware in the 1880s, depicted the frenzied world of Indian ritualistic dances on the handles of flatware. For inspiration he turned to *Catlin's Illustrations of the North American Indians.*

Tiffany's clients for Indian flatware included newspaper publishing king William Randolph Hearst, who ordered a service of 297 pieces.

This vase was presented in 1888 to Mr. Lewis May, president of New York City's Temple Emanu-El, in grateful recognition of his service. The Near Eastern flavor of the vase's form and decoration was inspired by traditional Judaic symbols and patternings.

Courtesy of Congregation Emanu-El of the City of New York

Elephant Tusk and Silver Cup

This dragon-handled trophy, carved from a single elephant tusk, is an almost exact replica of the Morgan Cup, won by J. P. Morgan's sloop *Volunteer* in 1887.

RIGHT

The Goelet Cup for Schooners Now in the New York Yacht Club, 1884

This most lavish and appealing of all nineteenth-century sea-racing cups was won by Latham Fish's schooner *Grayling* in 1884.

Neptune as a merman brandishes his trident from the bow of the trophy's fancifully garlanded and lanterned galleon, which is borne on the backs of six silver dolphins.

Height 18¾ inches (47.6 cm); length: 22 inches (55.9 cm)
Courtesy of America II

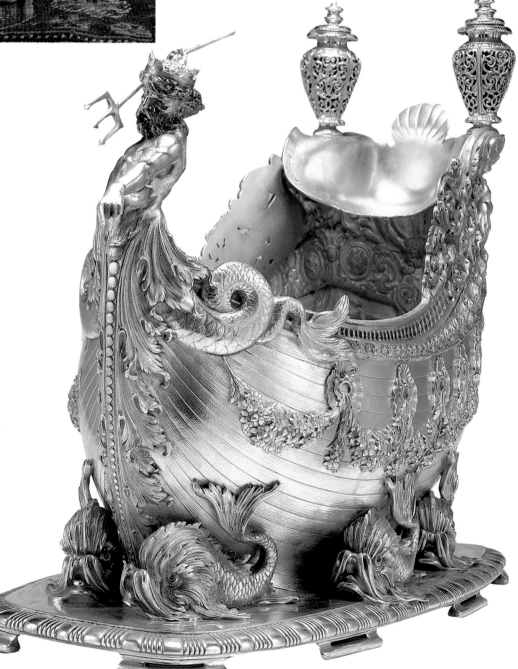

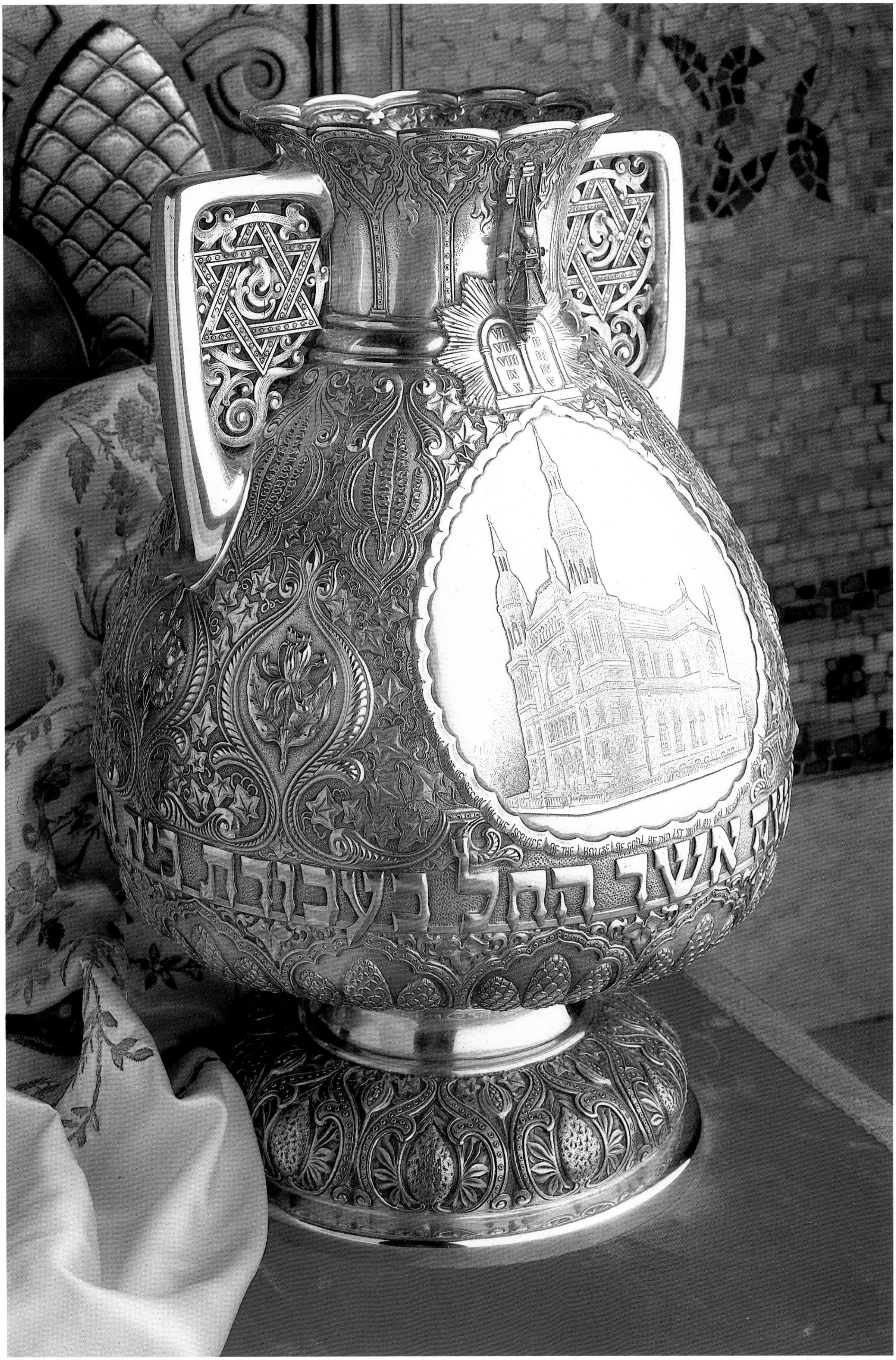

August Belmont II with Horse Memorabilia

Moneyed America's great fondness for horse racing in the second half of the nineteenth century was due largely to the avid support of the wealthy Belmont family. Their passion for horses is reflected in various Belmont trophies made by Tiffany's.

August Belmont II, seen in the above photograph, was possibly the most astute breeder of thoroughbreds in American racing history.

Beneath Belmont's photo is his letter to Tiffany's inviting its designers to his Long Island stables to draw and model the horses used in the design of the Belmont Cup.

The horse photos shown are from Tiffany's Design Archives and were used in the design.

The lead stirrup casting pattern was used for the handle of the now lost Belmont Tray.

OPPOSITE PAGE

The Belmont Cup

No horse-racing trophy is so celebrated as the August Belmont Memorial Cup, donated by the Belmont family in 1926 as a perpetual award for the Belmont Stakes, a race that was originated in 1867 by the multimillionaire banker August Belmont, then president of the Jockey Club.

Fenian, the first Belmont-owned horse to win the Stakes in 1869, is mounted on the cup's cover. The bowl, festooned with oak leaves and acorns, is supported by three other favorite thoroughbreds of August Belmont II, Hastings, Henry of Navarre, and Merry Prince.

Tiffany designers modeled the Belmont horses from life.

Height: 17½ inches (44.5 cm)
Belmont Stakes Trophy, courtesy of New York Racing Association, Inc.

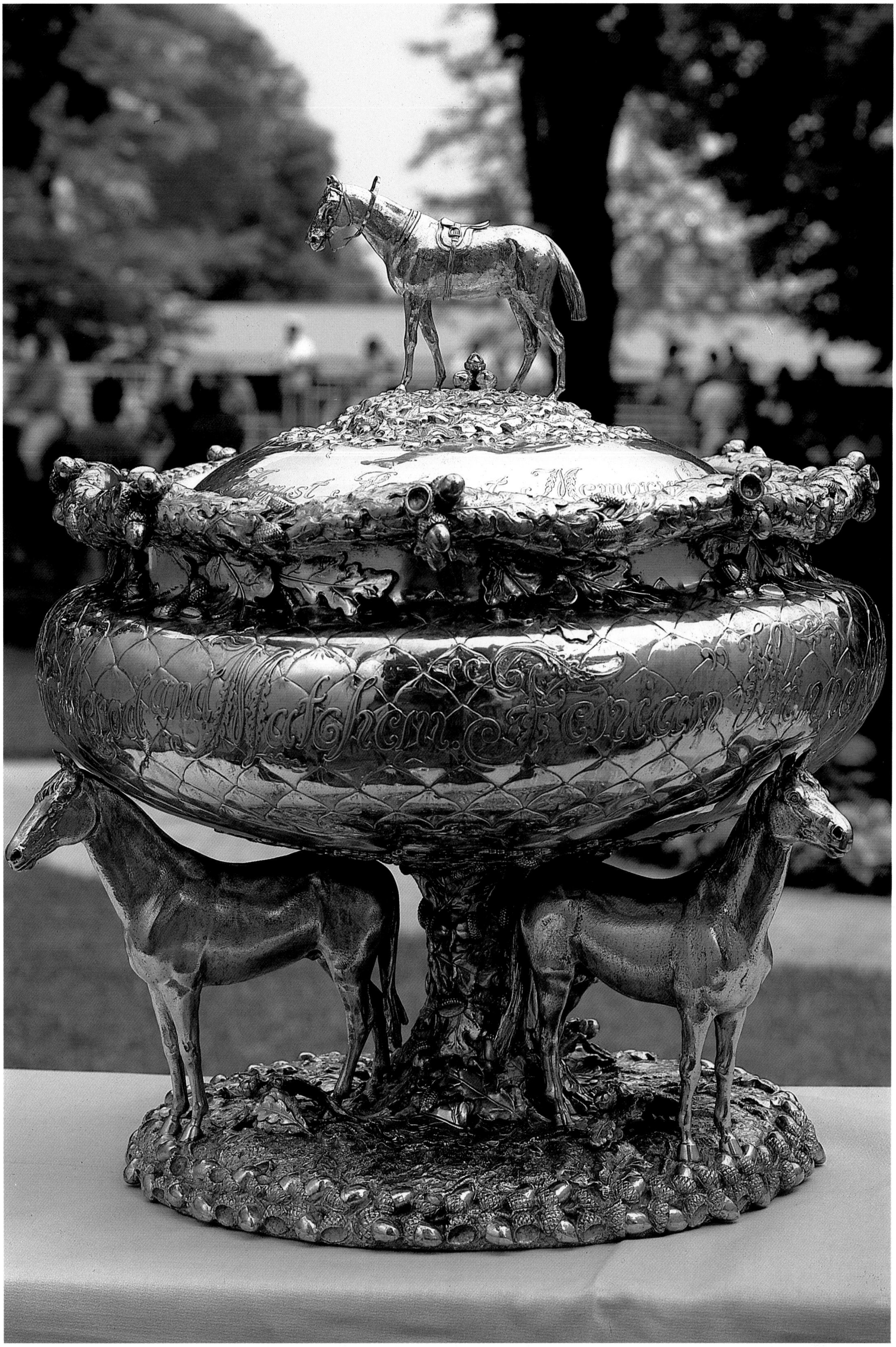

OPPOSITE PAGE
Thomas Webb Cameo Glass

The much-sought-after cameo glass from the English firm of Thomas Webb & Sons, like Tiffany's silverwear and jewels, consistently won awards at nineteenth-century world's fairs. The elaborately carved Webb pieces illustrated were specially ordered and retailed by Tiffany's. Mary Morgan, daughter of J. P. Morgan, designed the trumpet vase in the foreground.

The Empress Eugénie's Emerald, Diamond, and Pearl Brooch

Of European royalty, only Queen Elizabeth I of England had more jewels than Empress Eugénie, wife of Napoleon III of France. The illustrated brooch is part of the empress's great girdle, designed in 1864 by Alfred Bapst for the Empress to wear at a full-dress Fête Parée. In 1887, after the fall of the Second Empire, Eugénie fled France and the crown jewels were offered for public sale by the Ministry of Finance. Charles Tiffany bought over half a million dollars' worth of them—nine times the amount purchased by the next-highest bidder—and resold them to the Astors, the Herreras, and other heads of industrial America's "empires."

PAGE 84
Dresser from the Museum of the City of New York Holding a Collection of Tiffany-Bought Objects.

The opulence and exoticism of this ebonized dressing table echoes the Aesthetic Movement style of the objects on it. Such refined luxury goods were sold in prodigious quantity by Tiffany's to discerning shoppers in the 1880s.

Museum of the City of New York, the Rockefeller Bedroom

PAGE 85
Helen de Kay Diamond Pendant

Mounted with a 12¾-carat canary diamond, this heart-shaped Tiffany pendant belonged to Helen de Kay, whose handsome family fortune was acquired during the Civil War in the munitions industry. After the opening of the South African mines in 1860s, diamonds such as this became relatively plentiful, and Tiffany's designers worked at creating less visible settings, in order to draw attention to the quality of the stones themselves. The design search led to the universally acclaimed six-pronged "Tiffany setting" which was and remains the definitive diamond setting.

Tiffany's
Design Department compiled
albums of watercolor and
pencil drawings "from life" of
plants, flowers, and leaves to
serve as inspirations for its
silver and jewelry designs in
the late nineteenth-century.
The magnolia drawing shown
here comes from a series used
in 1893 in the design of the
Magnolia Vase now in the
Metropolitan Museum of Art.
The orchid drawings served
as models in the creation of
Tiffany's orchid jewelry
shown at the Paris Exposition
Universelle of 1889.

H. "2.3 Bicolor
Cutlega
Brazil

THIS DRAWING TO BE
RETURNED TO
TIFFANY & CO.
WHO RESERVE THE SOLE
RIGHT TO ESTIMATE
UPON IT.

*Enameled Orchid Jewelry from
Paris Exposition, 1889*

At the Paris
Exposition Universelle of
1889, Tiffany & Co.'s display
of enameled and jeweled gold
orchids made entirely of
American gold and gemstones
won the grand prize for
jewelry.

Created and shown in the
heyday of imperialism and
colonialism, these wonderfully
crafted jewels reflected the
popular mania for things
exotic and preferably tropical.

RIGHT
*Tiffany's Albums with Awards
and "Objets de Vertu" from
Various Expositions*

Only thirty
years after the founding of the
firm, Tiffany & Co. won its
first award of merit at the
Paris Exposition Universelle
of 1867. At the great world's
fairs of the last quarter of the
nineteenth century held in
Paris, Philadelphia, and
Chicago, the firm consistently
won the highest awards,
including fourteen grand
prizes in the Paris
expositions.

The gold, enamel, and
diamond floriform perfume
flask is typical of the
wonderfully designed and
crafted objects that won
Tiffany's such world acclaim.

BELOW
Wild Rose Watch in the
Collection of the Cooper-Hewitt
Museum, 1889

This exquisitely
executed gold, enamel, and
diamond floriform watch was
exhibited at the Paris
Exposition Universelle of
1889, where Tiffany's
received a gold medal for its
jewelry.

Cooper-Hewitt Museum, gift of Isabel
Shults, 1979

Mrs. Gould and Pearls, 1882

Few Belle
Époque actresses succeeded
in marrying their millionaire
admirers. Edith Kingdon did.
In 1886 she landed George
Gould, son of the great
financier Jay Gould, much to
the dismay of other Goulds.

Her good looks, remarkable
figure, and buoyant good
humor, all evident in this
series of photos of Mrs.
Gould posing with her new
pearls from Tiffany's,
eventually won over the
Goulds and New York
society.

OPPOSITE PAGE
Diamond Necklace, 1890–1900

This
Edwardian diamond necklace
is a fine example of the
splendid jewels that Tiffany's
provided in prodigious
quantity to the ladies of New
York society before World
War I.

Necklaces of this type with
coordinated tiaras and
earrings were so much the
uniform of Victorian and
Edwardian beauties who
graced the boxes of New
York's Metropolitan Opera
that the first tier at the Met
was, and still is, called the
"Diamond Horseshoe."

OPPOSITE PAGE
Nautilus Scent Bottle

The polluted air of nineteenth-century New York forced refined ladies to carry scent bottles. Tiffany's designed these precious objects in an almost limitless variety of shapes, sizes, and materials. The sumptuous example in the photograph, shown with working drawings for it and other Tiffany 1890s scent bottles, combines masterful chasing and enameling with precious stones and rock crystal. The flask epitomizes the opulence, invention, and elegance for which Tiffany's was famed.

Drawing, Tools from Tiffany's Silver Shop

When Charles T. Grosjean's still popular flatware pattern "Chrysanthemum" was introduced by Tiffany's in 1880, tea and coffee services and a number of trays and serving pieces were created to coordinate with Grosjean's wonderfully intricate and graceful design.

The Tiffany silver shop's still-used working drawing for a chrysanthemum soup tureen with casting patterns for its high-relief leaf and flower ornaments is shown here with silverworking tools.

OVERLEAF
Annealing Station in Tiffany's Silver Shop with Chrysanthemum Tureen

A "Chrysanthemum" soup tureen near completion in the annealing section of Tiffany's silver shop.

Casting Patterns, Tools, Dies, Chucks from Tiffany's Silver Shop, 1880

Many of the casting patterns, dies, spinning chucks, and silversmithing tools in daily use at Tiffany's silver factory date back over one hundred years.

The factory's many thousand intricately detailed lead and brass casting patterns for "fancy goods" comprise one of America's greatest collections of small-scale decorative sculpture.

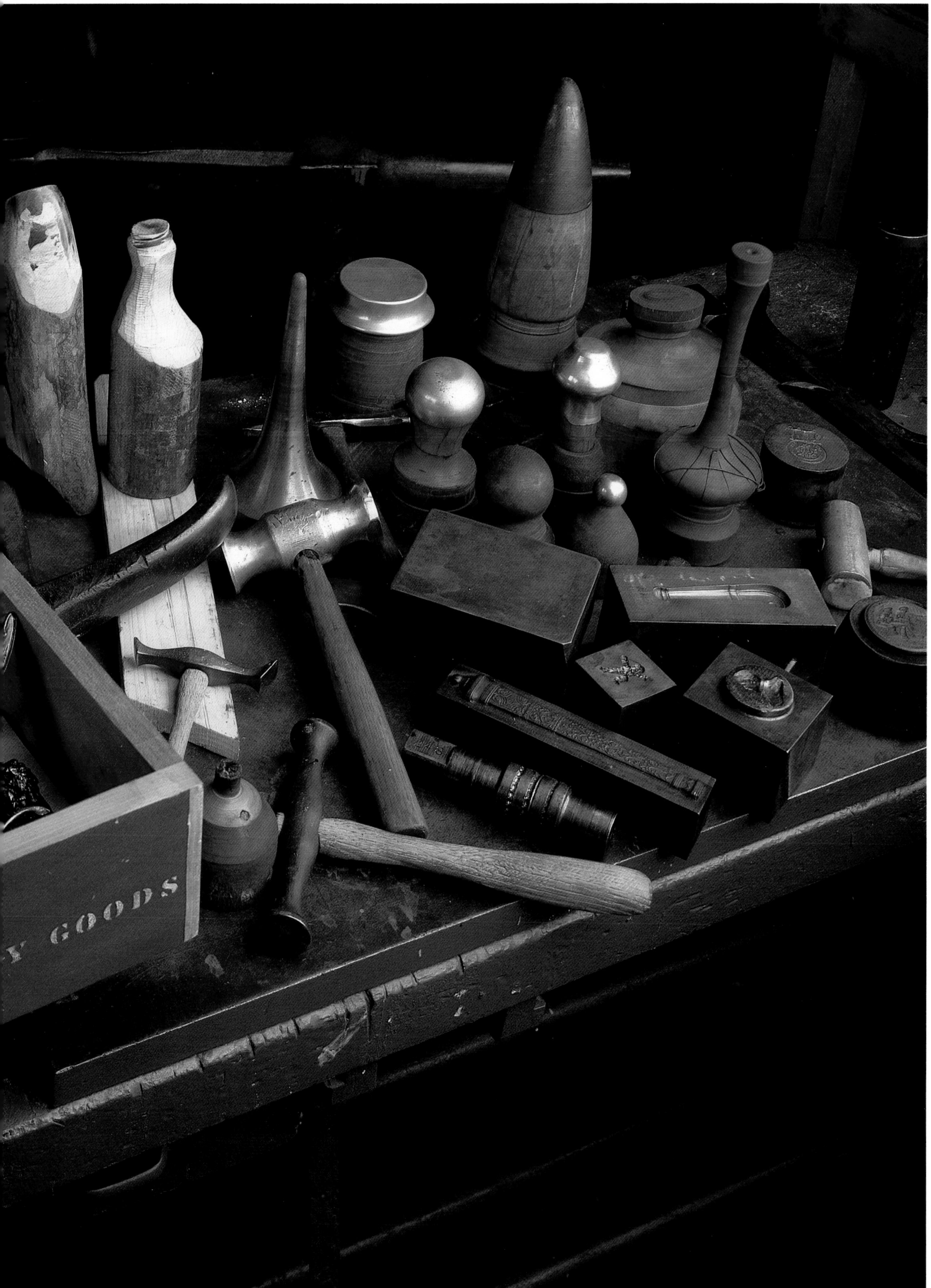
Y GOODS

OPPOSITE PAGE
Chrysanthemum Pitcher, 1893

This "Chrysanthemum" pitcher, exhibited in the Chicago World's Columbian Exposition of 1893, is a unique example of chasing and repoussé workmanship. To execute this decoration, the silversmith begins by roughing out the design from the interior with punches; he then fills the hollowed space with pitch; and lastly, he uses small chisels to "chase" the exterior surface.

LEFT
*Drawing for the Adams Vase
from the Tiffany Archives*

Designed by Paulding Farnham, the solid gold Adams Vase was presented to Edward Dean Adams by the American Cotton Oil Company in gratitude for having "saved the company from financial ruin." The foliate initials that cover the body of the vase in Farnham's preliminary drawing have been replaced in the final version by allegorical figures heroically celebrating Adams's financial successes.

The Metropolitan Museum of Art, gift of Tiffany & Co.

*Assortment of Tiffany Silver
Shown at the Chicago World's
Columbian Exposition of 1893*

This owl vase and the bat vase beside it were shown by Tiffany's at the Chicago World's Columbian Exposition of 1893, where Tiffany & Co. was awarded fifty-six medals for its superiority in every category of merchandise exhibited.

The watercolor and photos in the background show views of the Columbian Exposition's pavilions on the shore of Lake Michigan.

TIFFANY'S
150 YEARS

101

PRECEDING
Detail of the Adams Vase

Silver Pueblo Bowl, 1893

OPPOSITE PAGE
The Magnolia Vase

This most sumptuous Tiffany presentation piece, the Adams Vase, combines opulent Renaissance motifs with symbolic references to a simple American mainstay— the cotton plant. Approximately two hundred American semiprecious stones and pearls are encrusted in the intricately detailed surface of the nineteen-and-a-half-inch-high gold vase created by Tiffany's in 1893–1895.

Height: 19½ inches (49.5 cm); weight: 274 ounces
The Metropolitan Museum of Art, gift of Edward D. Adams, 1904

Tiffany's predilection for things American was evident before the turn of the century not only in the firm's extensive use of American gemstones and pearls but in its exploitation of the bold abstractions of American Indian design with its rich decorative possibilities.

This silver exhibition bowl inlaid with niello and copper takes its form from a Pueblo water basket and is ornamented with abstract Pueblo motifs.

It, along with other "Indian" silver pieces, was displayed at the Chicago World's Columbian Exposition of 1893.

The background drawings are from Tiffany's design albums of the period.

The splendid Magnolia Vase, measuring almost three feet in height and weighing nearly sixty-five pounds, was the most prominent and ambitious work exhibited by Tiffany & Co. at the Chicago World's Columbian Exposition of 1893. Made of silver with enamel, gold, and opal matrix inserts, the vase's shape was inspired by ancient Pueblo pottery and the eight handles around its neck by Toltec artifacts. These early American forms are combined with the vase's surface decoration of native American magnolias and other assorted flora to produce America's most opulent and remarkable piece of metalwork.

Height: 31 inches (78.8 cm)
The Metropolitan Museum of Art, gift of Mrs. Winthrop Atwell, 1899

As noted in Tiffany's 1893 "Blue Book," Russian enamels were a continuing favorite with Tiffany patrons at the turn of the century. These silver-gilt items were made for Tiffany & Co. by A. I. Kuzmichev, a Moscow firm noted for the exceptional quality of its enamel work. The style and technique employed exemplify the return in the second half of the nineteenth century to traditional native craft forms in Russia.

Chatelaine Watch

This late-nineteenth-century Tiffany chatelaine and pendant watch display the Victorian nostalgia for classical antiquity. Mythological figures of Aphrodite, her attendant goddesses, and Eroti are rendered in a painted enameling technique popular in late-nineteenth-century Europe for its resemblance to Roman cameos. The watch face is surrounded by rose diamonds set in 18-karat gold.

Favrile Glass Decanter and Cups

Of all America's achievements in the decorative arts, none has received more universal acclaim than Louis Comfort Tiffany's Favrile glass made between 1892 and 1928.

Inspired by the fluid forms and iridescent surfaces of ancient Middle Eastern and Roman glass, Tiffany's work is a triumph of Arts and Crafts Movement design.

The Favrile decanter set shown is typical of the Tiffany glass retailed at the firm's Fifth Avenue at Thirty-seventh Street store.

The Preservation Society of Newport County Collection, Kingscote, Newport, Rhode Island

Loving Cup in the Metropolitan Museum of Art, 1893

Combining amboyna wood, inlaid with mother-of-pearl and turquoise, with mountings of silver, this two-handled loving cup is representative of the exotic silver Tiffany's exhibited at the Chicago World's Columbian Exposition in 1893. Its curious shape was influenced by wooden Viking drinking vessels.

The Metropolitan Museum of Art, gift of Jack Steinberg, in memory of Mrs. Regina Perlmutter Steinberg, 1973

OVERLEAF
A Night at the Opera

During the Gilded Age, a public demonstration of interest in classical music and opera was one avenue to social acceptance. When railroad magnate William Henry Vanderbilt was reputedly excluded from the famous golden circle of the old Academy of Music, the operatic center of the city, he decided to build his own opera house. In 1863, with the help of several friends, including Jay Gould, he financed the elegant Metropolitan Opera at Thirty-ninth Street and Broadway and reserved five boxes exclusively for himself in the lavish first tier, the "Diamond Horseshoe." Tiffany's retailed many items for the operagoer, such as these mother-of-pearl opera glasses made by Tiffany's in the 1890s, the handsome engraved and etched pocket watch, and the fashionable silver-and-gold-mesh evening bag. Silver- and gold-handled canes were another Tiffany specialty

OPERA PROGRAM: *Courtesy of the Metropolitan Opera Archives*

PAGES 110–11
The Veterans' Room at the Armory

In 1880 the firm of Louis Comfort Tiffany and Associated Artists received their first major commission: the decoration of the Veterans' Room of the 7th Regiment Armory on New York's Park Avenue. Utilizing iron chains, metallic paints, iridescent glass tiles, and massive oak beams, Tiffany, the most brilliant interior designer of the latter half of the nineteenth century, created an at once opulent and severe masculine interior evocative of the pageantry of nineteenth-century warfare. In such surroundings, this table set with Tiffany Favrile glass and "Chrysanthemum" silver epitomizes the civilized rewards of peace, a more usual theme for Tiffany & Co.

The Veterans' Room of the Knickerbocker Grey's 7th Regiment Armory, New York

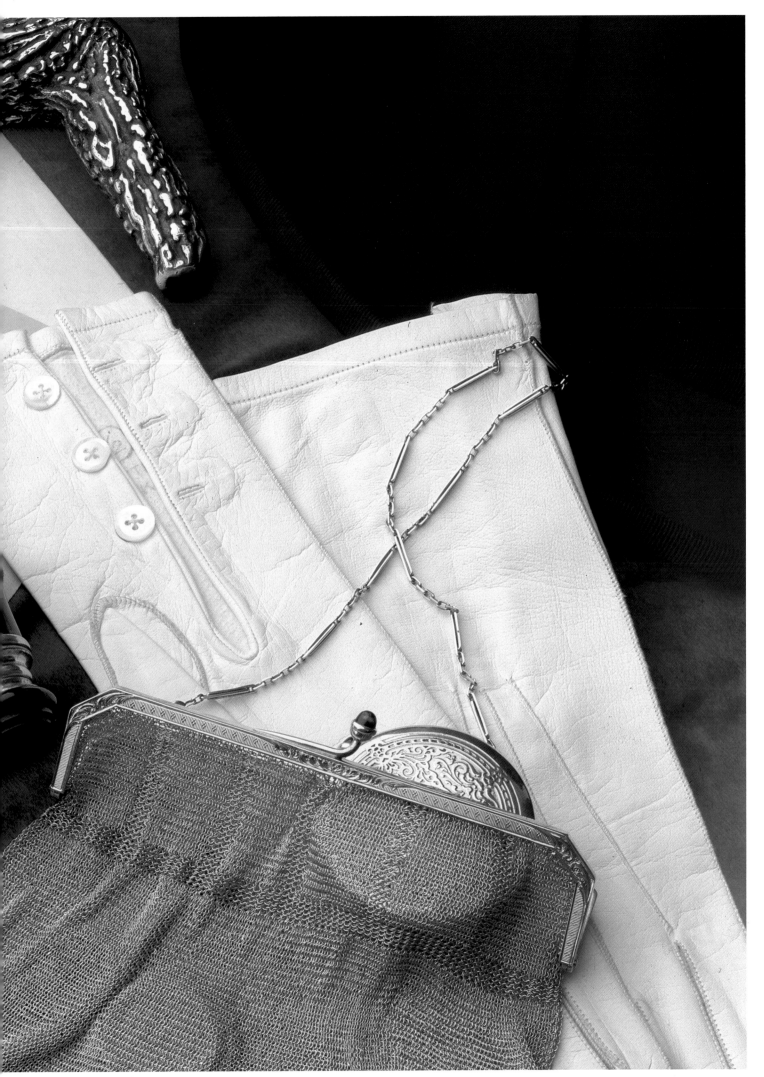

Cane Heads with Drawings

At the turn of
the century, the well-groomed
and fashionable American
gentleman owned several
walking sticks for the varied
occasions in his complex
social program. These status
symbols of their day typically
had simple gold or silver
mushroom handles; Tiffany's,
however, designed a

whimsical array of animal
heads, nautical and equestrian
motifs, or floral and foliate
pastiches to ornament the
canes of their more dapper
customers.

OPPOSITE PAGE

*The Flagler Vases, Museum of
the City of New York*

This tall,
elegant pair of silver vases,
accented with Art Nouveau
tendrils, was a present to
Annie Louise Lamont on her
marriage to Harry Harkness
Flagler, April 25, 1894.
Flagler, the son of oil
magnate Henry Morrison
Flagler, devoted his life to the

arts, reorganizing the
Symphony Society of New
York and its orchestra. He
was later president of the
Philharmonic Society.

*Museum of the City of New York, gift
of Harry Harkness Flagler*

OPPOSITE PAGE
Victorian Dresser

If Tiffany's provided nineteenth-century America with jewels and extravagant table wares for its social adventures and celebrations, it also provided luxurious accoutrements for more minor domestic rituals. Not least among these was the lady's dressing table where an innocent delight in glamour and elegance reigned, propped by richly ornamented silver clocks, dresser sets, picture frames, and vases all made in abundance by Tiffany's silversmiths.

Lillian Russell

To maintain her celebrated "hourglass" silhouette, New York's late-nineteenth-century musical stage queen Lillian Russell rode in Central Park on a sterling silver bicycle, reputedly offered by her close friend the flamboyant playboy Diamond Jim Brady. The story, however, is apocryphal. Brady, in fact, had a dozen bicycles gold-plated by another firm, as Tiffany's had refused his order, and gave them to friends.

Less celebrated admirers presented Russell with her Tiffany bicycle. The Tiffany frames hold photos of Russell, Brady, and the bicycle.

1900–1919

The dates of Charles Tiffany's leadership of Tiffany & Co. (1837–1902) coincided almost exactly with the dates of Queen Victoria's reign (1837–1901). She led her country from the post-Georgian Period through the Industrial Revolution into modern times.

Charles Tiffany set standards for commerce and the decorative arts in the same period. They both exited shortly after the turn of the century, ceding their worlds to the sophistication of Edwardianism and the uncertainties of the twentieth century.

The Tiffany & Co. Louis Comfort Tiffany inherited was a far cry from the small store founded by his father in the "frontier town" atmosphere of early-nineteenth-century New York.

Tiffany's moved to a grandly scaled stone-and-steel palace on Fifth Avenue designed by Stanford White. Here, as design director, the younger Tiffany encouraged traditions of design and craftsmanship and brought his own aesthetic of forms borrowed from nature with luminous color and richly elaborated surfaces.

From its new Venetian Renaissance Revival palace, Tiffany's supplied the Renaissance Revival styles that reflected capitalism's brawn and bite, and profited from the protean talents that had made Louis Comfort Tiffany America's most distinguished member of the Arts and Crafts Movement.

OPPOSITE PAGE
Painting of Charles L. Tiffany by William Merrit Chase, 1902

The great American Impressionist painter William Merritt Chase captures the vitality and creative genius of Charles Tiffany in this portrait painted in 1902. Tiffany was one of the greatest entrepreneurs and showmen America has ever known. By the end of the nineteenth century his unerring taste and understanding of the marketplace enabled Tiffany & Co. to grow from a small "Stationery and Dry Goods" store to the foremost retailer of luxury goods in America.

BELOW LEFT
Casting Patterns of Goblet and Ladle from the Lawson Cup

The Lawson Cup, a punch bowl with a ladle and eleven goblets, was presented by Thomas Lawson to the Hull-Massachusetts Yacht Club in 1901 as a prize for ninety-foot sloops. The illustrated lead casting patterns with their voluptuously seductive mermaids were the models used by Tiffany's silversmiths to create the ladle and handles for the goblets.

The "mermaids" are intriguingly suggestive of the expensive courtesans who played such important roles in forming nineteenth-century taste.

PAGE 117
Cut-Glass Dessert Service

Engraved crystal was already a popular gift item from Tiffany's at the turn of the century. This dessert service, made for Tiffany's by T. G. Hawkes Glass Company of Corning, New York, in the early part of this century, displays exceptional workmanship in the sculptural shading of its decoration

The
Renaissance Revival style was
wildly popular with New
Yorkers of means at the turn
of the century. This setting of
Tiffany silverware encrusted
with scrolling vegetation and
inhabited by armies of *putti*
was quite familiar to the
period's successful Wall Street
brokers and bankers and their
families. Tiffany's
"Olympian" silver flatware,
introduced in 1880, would
undoubtedly have been found
on the dinner tables of the
proud possessors of this
handsomely chased wine
bucket.

OVERLEAF
*Art Pottery Designed by Louis
Comfort Tiffany*

Nothing
encapsulates the spirit of the
Arts and Crafts Movement in
the final quarter of the
nineteenth century so
completely as Art Pottery,
which united the elements of
earth, water, and fire with a
time-honored craft.

Louis Comfort Tiffany was,
not surprisingly, a leader in
the field. Not only did his
Tiffany Studios provide
leaded art-glass lampshades
for the handsome "cucumber
green" glazed vases of Greuby
Potteries, but Tiffany
produced in his studios a
series of floriform Art
Nouveau vases whose
refinement and intricacy of
line, joined with an
extraordinary subtlety of
coloring, place them among
the most sophisticated
achievements of the American
Arts and Crafts Movement.

*Medals presented to
J. P. Morgan*

Banker,
financier, art collector, and
yachtsman John Pierpont
Morgan (1837–1913) is
pictured here in full nautical
regalia in 1897, the year of
his election as commodore of
the New York Yacht Club.
These bronze, gold, silver,
and silver-gilt decorative and
commemorative medals
presented to Morgan were all
made by Tiffany's. They
include the oval committee
medal of a schooner

presented at the one hundred
and forty-second annual
banquet of the New York
State Chamber of Commerce
and the silver commemorative
medal given in observance of
the first half century of the
Cooper Union in 1909.

*Archives of The Pierpont Morgan
Library, New York*

OPPOSITE PAGE
*Casting Patterns and
Photographs of Tiffany
Presentation Pieces*

These winged
Japanese dragon patterns for
the handles on the Charles
M. Schwab Cup, made in
1901, are from Tiffany's vast
collection of lead casting
patterns. Such patterns were
used to make the often
eccentric finials, handles,
spouts, feet, and variety of
arbitrary protuberances that
so richly and imaginatively
ornamented Tiffany's silver.

PRECEDING OVERLEAF
*Georgian Revival Silver
Centerpiece*

Completed on
April 30, 1904, this silver
centerpiece in George III
Revival style is a masterful
example
of Tiffany's silversmithing.
Weighing thirty-three and a
half pounds, the piece has an
extravagantly lap-over-edge
intricately chased and pierced
with foliate scrolls.

*Detail of Vegetable Dish
Designed by Paulding
Farnham*

The Victorian
period found a seemingly
endless fascination with
Italiante design. This covered
silver vegetable dish-cum-
centerpiece designed by
Tiffany's Paulding Farnham
displays all the proliferation
of sphynxes, *putti*, urus,
scrolls, and volutes so dear to
the Renaissance Revival.

*Tray and Shovel
Commemorating the New York
Subway System*

Upon
completion of the subway
system in 1904, the New York
City Rapid Transit Railroad
Commissioners presented this
massive Tiffany silver tray to
August Belmont, president of
the Rapid Transit Subway
Construction Company. The
design speaks of the
tremendous pride New
Yorkers felt in what then
seemed a miraculous
achievement.

The commemorative spade,
decorated with the arms of
the City of New York, was
used by Mayor Robert A. Van
Wyck to shovel the first
spadeful of earth at the
subway excavation site on
March 24, 1900.

*TRAY: Museum of the City of New
York, gift of August Belmont*

*SPADE: Museum of the City of New
York, gift of Mrs. William Van Wyck*

The Flagler Mirror, 1902

This elaborately
scrolled and garlanded Louis
XV Revival mirror, tied with
bows and inhabited by a trio
of *putti*, was made by
Tiffany's in 1902 for Mary
Lily Keenan, third wife of
Henry Morrison Flagler, co-
founder of Standard Oil and
the developer of the eastern
coast of Florida.

The Henry Morrison Flagler Museum

The Yale Mace, 1903

The Yale Mace, designed and given to the university by Professor Samuel S. Sanford of the Department of Music, has been carried in academic processions by the chief marshall since 1905. Of silver gilt and weighing twenty-four pounds, the mace is embellished with symbolic references to virtue, including oak, ivy, and Yale's own elm leaves. Four figures, symbolizing Art, Science, Law, and Theology, stand on the rim of the cup.

Yale University

OPPOSITE PAGE
Drawings of Class Rings

Class rings were first introduced at the United States Naval Academy in 1869; however, it was not until 1899 that an official inscription was designed by Park Benjamin, a former graduate. On the official insignia, a hand grasping a trident rests above a shield depicting an ancient galley ship and an open book. Around the shield are torches, symbols of knowledge and wisdom, while beneath appears the inscription Ex SCIENTIA TRIDENS (From Knowledge, Sea Power).

The Tiffany drawings date from 1898 to 1917. Each of these elaborte rings is set with an oval gemstone, surrounded on either side by the Academy insignia and the individual class insignia, designed each year by the current graduating class.

OVERLEAF
Traveling Case

Compact, useful, and elegant, this personalized lady's traveling dressing case exemplifies Tiffany's provision for personal luxury on all occasions.

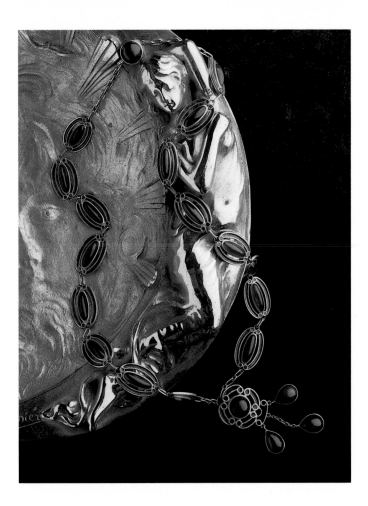

This rare, forty-two-inch-high Art Nouveau figural clock in doré bronze was sculpted exclusively for Tiffany & Co. by French artist Marcel Début and cast by Keller Frères in Paris around 1905. The fluid contours of the swirling drapery rise to enfold three nude female figures, who support and encircle the clock. The sculptured bronze clock face is typical of Tiffany clock dials of the period.

Courtesy of the Paul Singer Foundation

*Jade, Gold, and Enamel
Necklace*

With the encouragement of the Arts and Crafts Movement, a desire for simple jewelry forms made with semiprecious stones such as jade came into vogue at the turn of the century. This necklace of linked jade lozenges surrounded by green enamel on a gold framework was sold at Tiffany's in the first quarter of the twentieth century. Its curvilinear forms reflect the influence of Art Nouveau and, of course, of Louis Comfort Tiffany, who undoubtedly oversaw its design.

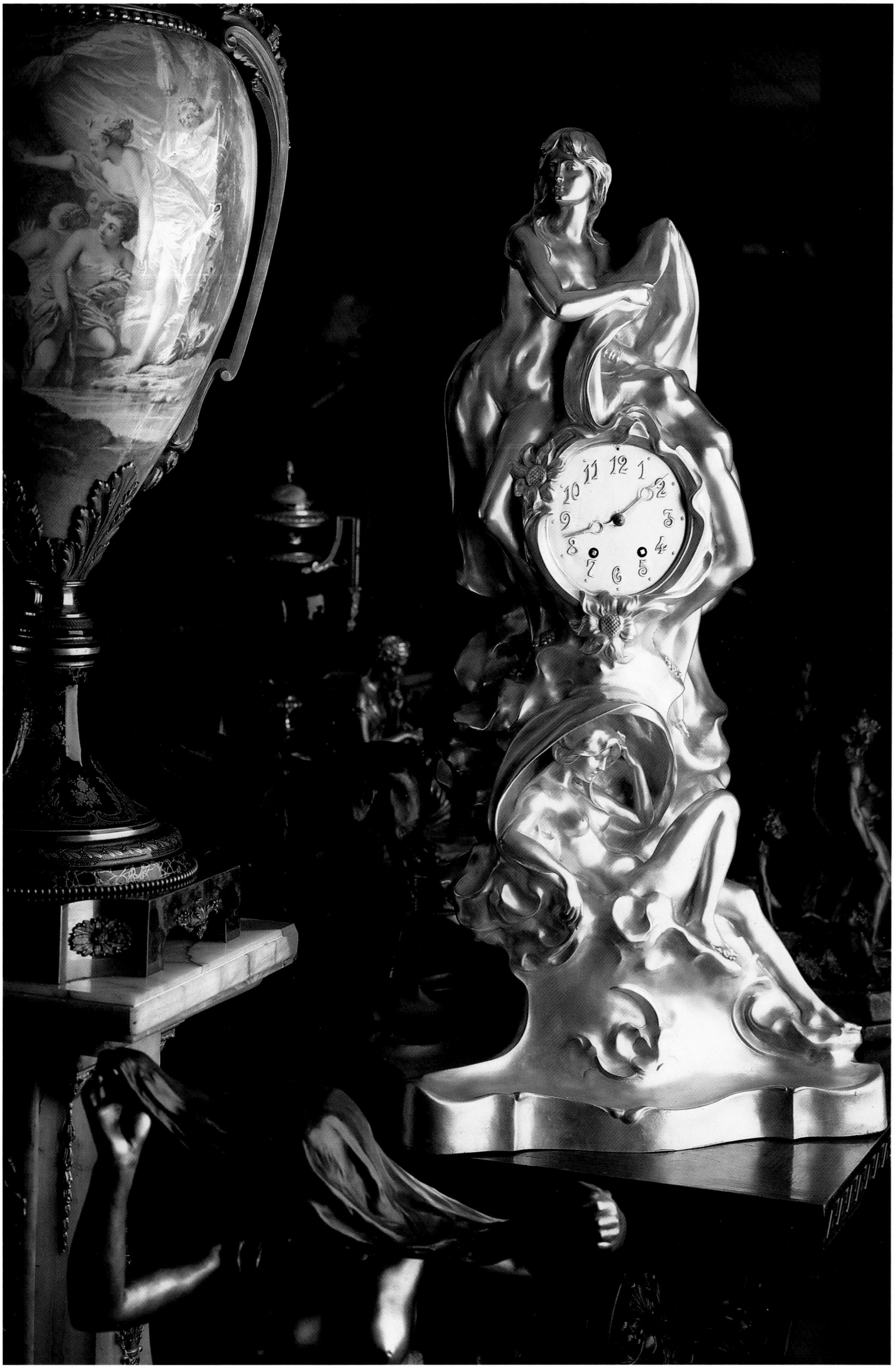

Enamel Demitasse Set

This after-dinner coffee service, set with zircons and essonite garnets, was exhibited at the Pan-American Exposition in Buffalo in 1901. The overall encrustations of interlocking design are in the Celtic Revival style, one of the more whimsical if lesser known of the late nineteenth century's many "revivals," but one used with distinction by Tiffany's silversmiths and jewelers.

Collection of the Newark Museum

18-Karat-Gold Demitasse Set,
Inset with Citrines

It was not
uncommon around the turn
of the century for Tiffany's
clients to order tea and coffee
services in solid gold rather
than in the more traditional
sterling silver. The Art
Nouveau-style foliate
decorations of this 18-karat-
gold early-twentieth-century
Tiffany coffee set inset with
faceted citrines is surprisingly
restrained, considering its
materials.

This Neo-
classical Revival style, 18-karat
gold tea set was designed in
1904 for Henry Morrison
Flagler and was proudly
displayed by Flagler's third
wife, Mary Lily Keenan, in
their seventy-four-room
mansion in Palm Springs.
Mr. Flagler, not so fond of
formal teas and other social
gatherings as his wife, is
reported to have "built
himself secret stairwells so
that he could easily slip out
of parties and retire to sleep
or read."

The Henry Morrison Flagler Museum

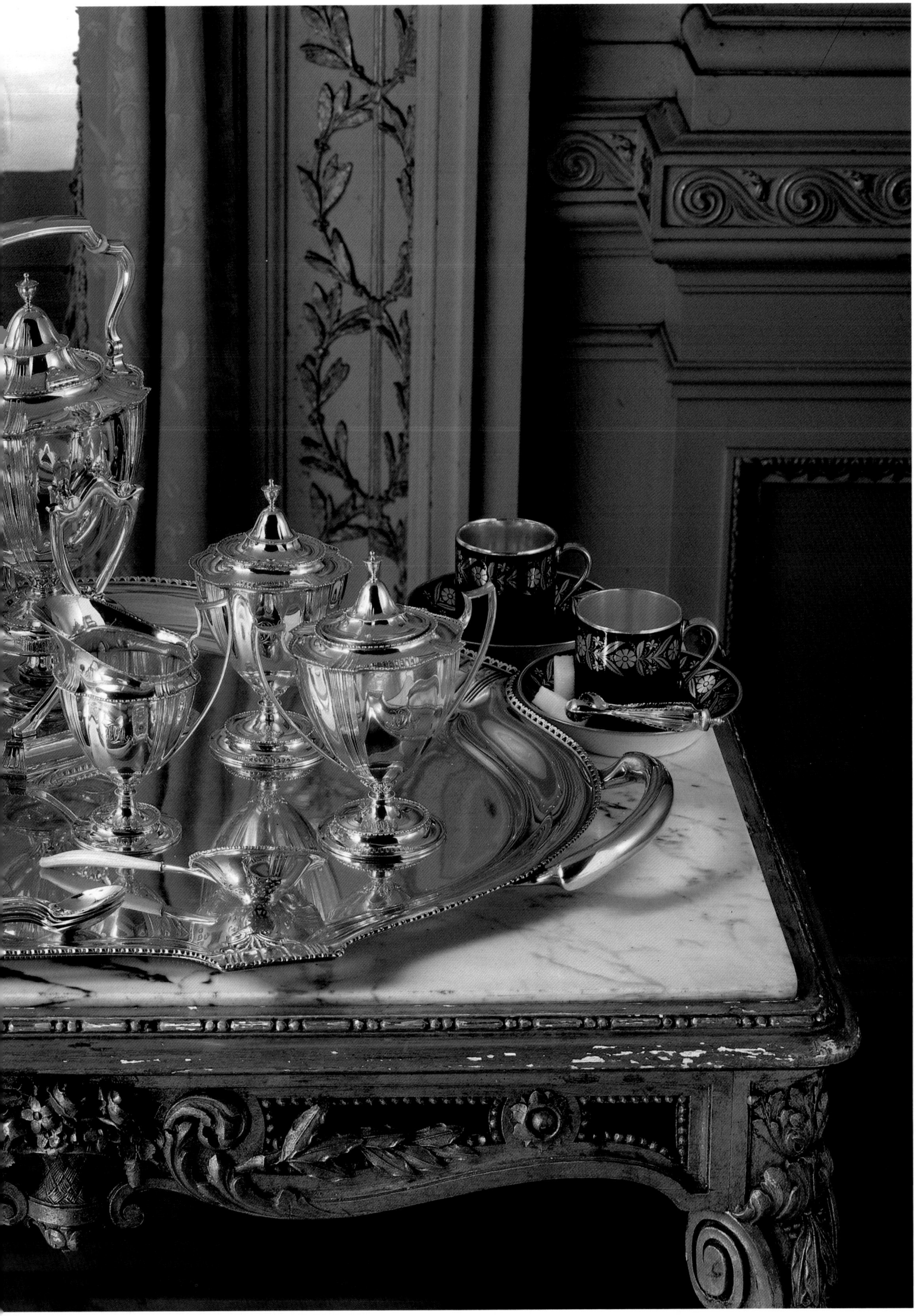

Cigarette Case, 1900

Prettily set with grape-colored sapphires, this gold cigarette case reflects the opulence and period charm of the Edwardian Age, when such objects were common dress accessories sold in large volume by Tiffany's.

It sits on a 1900 drawing from Tiffany's Archives for the accompanying match safe.

BELOW
Bee Brooch

Jeweled insects, such as this pearl-and-diamond bee made by Tiffany's around 1885, were a fad that reached New York in the 1860s when ladies scattered them liberally about their hair and bonnets and corsages. The fashion for bees and dragonflies, ladybugs and butterflies continued through the Edwardian period and is alive and well today.

OPPOSITE PAGE
Jewelry Designed by Louis Comfort Tiffany

Louis Comfort Tiffany believed that each piece of jewelry "acts as a little missionary of art and tries in its own dumb way to convert the Philistine." The special Tiffany Art Jewelry department set up in 1902 under his direction sold his innovative designs that combined enameling with multicolored gems. His mannered and stylish designs often echoed Celtic, Medieval, Byzantine, and Oriental patterns and were set with stones chosen for their intriguing colors rather than their intrinsic value.

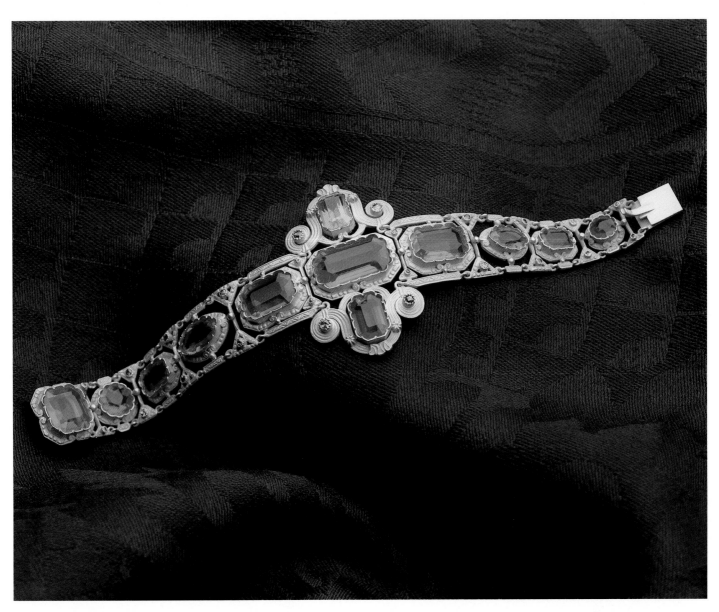

OPPOSITE PAGE
Chrysanthemum Brooch, 1904

In the last quarter of the nineteenth century freshwater pearling became popular in the Mississippi River valley. The river then yielded an unusually large number of irregular pearls of superb quality such as the "dogtooth" pearls used to form petals in this extraordinary chrysanthemum brooch.

The use of native American pearls in Tiffany jewelry was encouraged by the company's renowned gemologist, Dr. George Kunz, who always championed native American gems.

Fire Opal Bracelet Owned by Gypsy Rose Lee

This strikingly bold bracelet, set with Mexican fire opals and scattered with green demantoid garnets, is characteristic of Tiffany's fondness for a bold use of colored stones in its jewels. The bracelet was given to the legendary and much loved queen of burlesque Gypsy Rose Lee in the 1940s by her husband.

PAGE 144
Moonstone Pendant Watch

A carved moonstone portrait of Night, who, with diamond wings unfurled, rests her head on a star-studded diamond cushion in this delightfully inventive pendant watch created by Tiffany's jewelry designers at the turn of the century.

PAGE 145
Enameled Watch Pendant

The extremes of refinement sought by the Edwardians are evident in the delicate, almost fragile lines and decorations of this pre-World War I Tiffany pendant watch in enamel, rock crystal, platinum, and diamonds.

1920–1949

When the French Government invited the United States to exhibit at the Exposition des Arts Décoratifs in 1925, the Calvin Coolidge administration declined, saying there were no decorative arts in the United States.

This was inaccurate. Tiffany & Co. could well have exhibited as it had in all past Paris expositions; but it was true that 1920s America had not yet assimilated the modernist ideas formulated by pre-World War I *Wiener Werkstaette* designers or the post-World War I Bauhaus group that so influenced European design and heralded the Art Deco style.

Louis Comfort Tiffany never departed from the tenets of Art Nouveau or, as it is often called, "the Tiffany style," and that style had little sympathy with modernism.

He knew, however, how to maintain and promote his company's image as America's guardian of taste. In his mansion on the corner of Seventy-second Street and Madison Avenue and in his fanciful villa, Laurelton Hall at Oyster Bay, he set an example of stylishness, elegance, and privilege in the flamboyant dinners, balls, and diversions he offered his friends and clients. His guests drank from iridescent Tiffany Favrile glasses in exotically ornamented rooms lit by Tiffany glass fixtures. But, in his store, he offered his clients objects whose design was beginning to show the elegant restraint associated with the modern Tiffany's.

In the year of the New York World's Fair, 1939, Tiffany & Co. decided to move twenty blocks up Fifth Avenue from its Venetian palace to a sleek new building designed by Cross & Cross in high American Art Deco style at the corner of Fifty-seventh Street and Fifth Avenue. The pure lines and harmonious proportions of its steel, marble, and limestone façade, pierced by vaultlike steel doors and small, theatrically lit shadow-box display windows, announced the enchanted world of rare and precious jewels within.

Tiffany's designs of the Second World War and postwar years shared the tailored, streamlined look of the period. With their suave, polished surfaces and their machine-precise lines, they gave definition to the popular term "elegant simplicity."

OPPOSITE PAGE
The Lipton Cup, 1930

After Sir Thomas Lipton's fifth and final attempt to win back the America's Cup for England, the humorist Will Rogers solicited funds from all Americans to present "the Gamest Loser in the World of Sports" with his own "loving" cup. The 18-karat-gold Lipton cup, made by Tiffany's, stands on a silver base and is decorated with shamrock leaves representing the series of *Shamrock* challengers (his fifth boat of that name is pictured in the distance) with which Lipton consistently lost the historic race.

Glasgow Museums and Art Galleries, Glasgow, Scotland

Shamrock V, Museum of Yachting, Newport, Rhode Island (in background)

PAGE 147
Dog Brooch 1940s

Drawing for platinum and diamond pavé brooch from Tiffany's Archives.

OVERLEAF
King's Cup Keepers

In 1912 the King's Cup was given by King George V of England to the New York Yacht Club as a sailing prize. These seven "keepers" made by Tiffany's were won by Cornelius Vanderbilt's great-grandson Harold Vanderbilt during the 1920s and 1930s. Harold Vanderbilt also successfully defended the America's Cup three times. His "keepers" are shown here on the balustrade of the Vanderbilts' Marble House in Newport, where both the King's Cup races and America's Cup races were traditionally held.

The Preservation Society of Newport County, from the Harold S. Vanderbilt Collection, Marble House, Newport, Rhode Island

Its association with purity has guaranteed silver an important role in Christian liturgy. This silver-gilt monstrance from St. Patrick's Cathedral in New York was designed in 1942 to accompany the Exposition Throne for the new main altar. Modeled by Tiffany's in the shape of a Celtic cross with an interlacing sunburst encircling the crossing arms, it stands forty inches high and is set with twenty-two amethysts.

St. Patrick's Cathedral, New York City

Harry Houdini's Watch

The escapes from handcuffs, chains, strait jackets, and underwater tanks by the great American magician Harry Houdini are legendary.

At the conclusion of an eleven-week run at Keith's Theater in Boston on April 19, 1922, Paul Keith gave "the man who could walk through steel walls" this enameled and diamond-studded Tiffany pocket watch with a specially designed chain of miniature gold handcuffs.

OPPOSITE PAGE
Art Deco Travel Clock

Pearl Stringing

This small
Tiffany Art Deco travel clock
was made in the 1930s of
enameled gold with diamond
hands and numbers.

Its crisp and elegant lines,
its rich colors and surfaces,
and its highly stylized floral
motifs make it a fine example
of the suave and dapper
objects sold by Tiffany's in
the Art Deco period.

Tiffany's was
once America's greatest dealer
of natural Oriental pearls, one
of society's favorite symbols of
wealth until their astronomic
prices were eroded by the
success of cultured pearls.

Fine cultured pearls are
strung and set into jewelry
today, just as their cousins
pictured here in Tiffany's
albums of the 1880s were
over a hundred years ago.

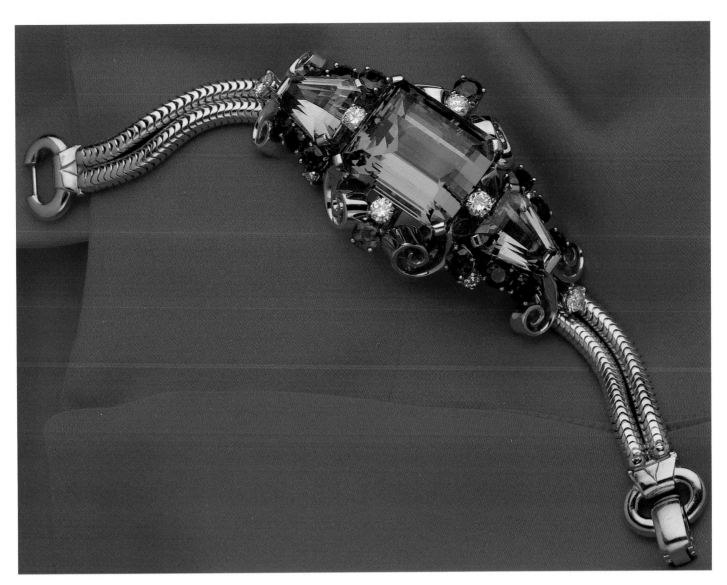

OPPOSITE PAGE
Art Deco Vanity Case

Aquamarine Bracelet

In a 1936 issue of *Vogue,* this silver toilet set was advertised by Tiffany's as "the latest luxury to put on your dressing table—a glorified vanity-box." Equipped with a mirror, brush, comb, jewel case, powder and cream containers, the Art Deco vanity set is a sleek, modern counterpart of the lavish and elaborate toilet services produced in seventeenth- and eighteenth-century Europe. Like them, the Tiffany vanity box signaled a lady's taste and wealth.

Generously scaled and vividly colored stones became fashionable in jewelry of the late 1930s and the 1940s. To complement the "blond" look, aquamarines such as these fine-colored Brazilian stones, probably from the Santa Maria mine, were especially popular. The tubular snake chains holding them were much in favor in the period's designs.

1950–1987

In the mid-1950s another great American merchant, Walter Hoving, took over Tiffany & Co. His first act was to appoint a new design director, Van Day Truex, to continue the Tiffany tradition of finest design.

Under Hoving's leadership, many of the greatest jewelry designers of the twentieth century came to work at Tiffany's: Jean Schlumberger, Donald Claflin, Elsa Peretti, Angela Cummings, and Paloma Picasso.

Tiffany's precious gem department, headed by Louis Comfort Tiffany's great-grandson, Henry B. Platt, introduced to the world two new gemstones, tanzanite and tsavorite, and popularized George Kunz's discovery, kunzite.

Gene Moore, master of all he displays, was brought in to create the famous Tiffany's windows; the annual series of six tablesetting shows with their opening "Breakfast at Tiffany's" parties were launched; a Corporate Sales Division was established and branch stores opened across the country.

Hoving proved to be Charles Tiffany's equal as entrepreneur and showman. When he retired in 1981, he left Tiffany's some twenty times larger than he had found it and still a world symbol of quality and style.

In the early 1980s Tiffany's was briefly owned by a publicly held conglomerate; but, in 1984, under the leadership of its current chairman, William R. Chaney, it regained its independence. Today Tiffany's endures as it has for one hundred and fifty years as a testament to American taste and talent.

In 1967 a Masai tribesman unearthed a rare transparent blue zoasite—the first "new" blue gemstone to have been found in two thousand years. Mr. Henry Platt, great-grandson of Louis Comfort Tiffany and president of Tiffany's at the time, successfully promoted the newly discovered stones as a "Tiffany" gem. Platt named it "tanzanite" for its country of origin, Tanzania.

The 96.42-carat tanzanite in this diamond necklace is of exceptionally fine color, clarity, and brilliance and is typical of the extraordinary stones that Platt brought to prominence.

Elsa Peretti, a world-famous model and designer of perfume bottles and accessories for Halston, joined Tiffany's in 1974. All of her superbly elegant, stylish, and deceptively simple creations, whether jewelry, crystal, ceramics, or leather, are designed with an assured, smooth-flowing, organic line and structure.

This frontispiece in the Tiffany "Blue Book" of 1950 illustrates, along with other Tiffany jewels, a magnificent 75-carat emerald.

The catalogue caption reads:

"The 75 carat emerald set with diamonds in the brooch is remarkable for the superb color and clarity so rare in a stone of this size. It was cut from the heart of a much larger stone worn as a belt buckle by the Sultan of Turkey, Abdül-hamīd."

The catalogue price in 1950 was only $39,000.

OVERLEAF
Schlumberger Collage

The great twentieth-century French genius of jewelry design Jean Schlumberger began his career designing costume jewelry for Elsa Schiaparelli. He joined Tiffany's in 1956 and redefined fashionable jewelry for America. His fantastic designs played with tradition, innovatively combining both precious and semiprecious stones with enamel and drawing on the treasure trove of nature's own fantasies for inspiration.

JASMINE NECKLACE OF MULTICOLORED STONES AND DIAMONDS: *Collection of Mr. and Mrs. Milton Petrie*

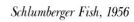

Schlumberger Fish, 1956

"I want to capture the irregularities of the universe. I observe nature and find verve," said Schlumberger.

Donald Claflin,
Strawberry Ensemble

Donald Claflin
was one of Tiffany's principal
jewelry designers in the late
1960s and early 1970s. He
brought exoticism, whimsy,
and charm to his designs'
essentially classic foundations.

This strawberry ensemble
was fashioned from carved
coral, surrounded by
diamond-studded leaves.
Collection of Mrs. Walter Matthau

OPPOSITE PAGE
Schlumberger Iguana Clip

Purchased by
Richard Burton as a gift for
his wife Elizabeth Taylor, this
large dolphin clip designed
by Jean Schlumberger was
dubbed the "Iguana" by
Burton, who had just
completed filming *The Night
of the Iguana.*
Collection of Miss Elizabeth Taylor

PAGE 170
The Johnson China

Breaking with
the formality of previous
White House china services,
Mrs. Lyndon Johnson
commissioned Tiffany & Co.
in the late 1960s to design a
porcelain service decorated
with American wildflowers,
motifs which reflected her
four-year crusade for the
beautification of America.
The service was designed by
Van Day Truex, whose only
concession to officialdom was
an American eagle at the
center of the service plate.
Truex's eagle was adapted
from the White House china
of President James Madison.
*White House Collection, the White
House*

PAGE 171
The Super Bowl Trophy

No sporting
event attracts more spectators
than the annual Super Bowl.
Designed in 1966 by Tiffany
& Co., the Super Bowl
trophy was recently renamed
the Vince Lombardi Trophy
as a tribute to this coach who
epitomized excellence in
football.

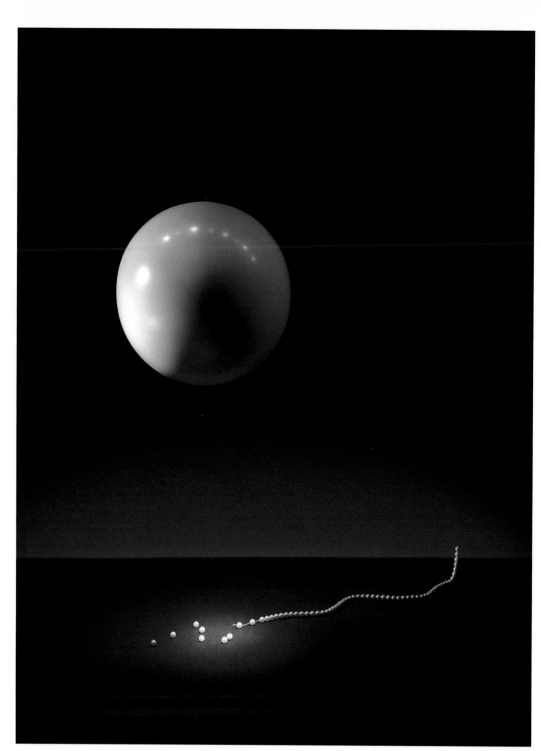

Witty, arresting, fanciful, and delightfully provocative, the enchanted microcosms of Gene Moore's Tiffany windows have been a prime attraction of Fifth Avenue since 1955.

The unexpected meetings and minglings of eggshells and emeralds, umbrellas and watches, shoes and Schlumberger boxes, saws and champagne glasses, fishhooks and solitaires, ice cream cones and diamonds in Moore's windows take Tiffany's shoppers into a world of privilege and magic.

*Angela Cummings Leaf
Necklace*

Angela
Cummings designed jewelry
for Tiffany's from 1967 to
1983. Her lyrical designs were
anything but traditional,
combining unusual stones
and materials such as wood
and gold and diamonds, steel
and gold, hematite and
diamonds, or gold with silver
and copper. Her inspiration
came from nature, as seen in
this multicolored necklace of
autumn leaves, fashioned
from gold and copper.

OPPOSITE PAGE
*Elsa Peretti "Bone" Cuff
Bracelet, 1974*

The
triumphant revival of silver
jewelry in the 1970s and
1980s was led by the highly
sensual, sculptural, and
original work of Elsa Peretti
for Tiffany's.

The "Peretti Open Heart,"
her "Equestrian" belt buckle,
the "Peretti Bean," and her
"Bone" cuff bracelet (shown
here) stand among the finest
and most successful designs
of the twentieth century.

PAGE 176
Van Day Truex

Van Day Truex
was a quintessential designer,
exerting a powerful influence
on style, first as president of
the Parsons School of Design
and later as Design Director
of Tiffany & Co. His
reverence for the past,
particularly the spirit of the
eighteenth century, was
combined with a love of
natural forms. Truex replaced
"the faceless, the negative, the
so-called 'modern' look" with
fresh new images that
possessed grace and
imagination. His works range
from the elaborate two

hundred and fifty place
settings designed for the
White House during the
Johnson administration to his
"Rock Cut" crystal pieces, his
"Seed Pod" silver centerpiece,
Baccarat "Bordeaux Bottle,"
"Dionysus" decanter
(included in the Museum of
Modern Art's Design
Collection), and Tiffany's
"Bamboo" flatware, which
won the 1966 A.I.D.
International Design Award
for silver.

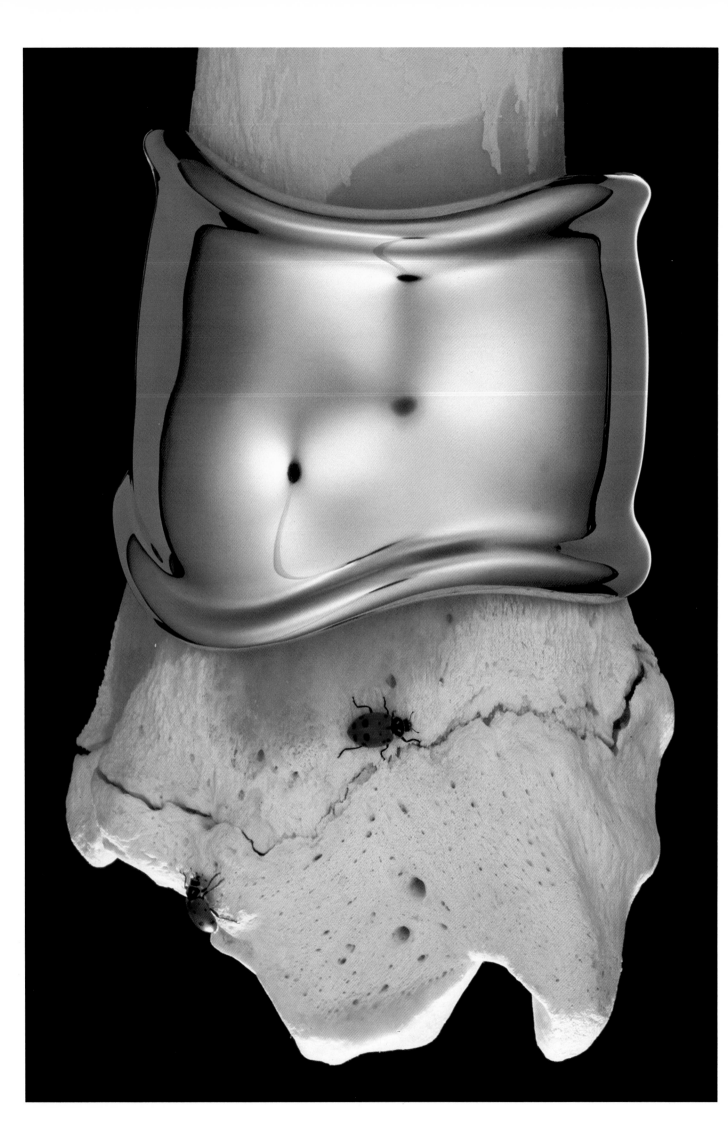

TIFFANY TASTE
By John Loring
Doubleday & Company, Inc.
TIFFANY & Co.

Since 1979 designer, artist, and writer John Loring has led forward the great aesthetic traditions of Tiffany & Co. as its Design Director and arbiter of taste.

A natural simplicity joined by vigor, imagination, and stylishness underlies his work as seen here in some of his diverse designs: the "Atlas" Watch; "Halcyon" Private Stock porcelain; "Madison" and "Nemours" crystal; the double-walled silver bowl; "swivel" clock; and the crab-and-sea-urchin vermeil candlesticks

Tiffany's table settings are almost as well known as Tiffany jewelry and have drawn crowds to the New York store since 1956. A pure if casual delight in luxury is the keynote of this setting, which includes Tiffany's hand-colored Mason's Ironstone "Yellow Flowers," "King William" silver flatware, and bold cut-crystal old-fashioned and highball glasses in Tiffany's "Madison" pattern. The setting is lit by "Twinelight" candleholders, whimsically molded in the shapes of balls of twine.

Strongly colored gems set in boldly scaled, tailored settings characterize Paloma Picasso's creations. The large colored stones in the illustrated minaudières and bangle bracelets contrast dramatically with the voluminous, highly polished gold surfaces and typify the Paloma Picasso style.

Tiffany's distinctive inlaid "Allures" jewelry utilizes colored semiprecious stones cut to precision, in a manner similar to mosaic work. Coral, black jade, lapis, mother-of-pearl, turquoise, amethyst, opal, and hematite create seductive interplays of color and suave surfaces.

"Tiffany Allures" patterns, in the Tiffany tradition, are drawn from nature as well as from classic American Indian and Japanese motifs.

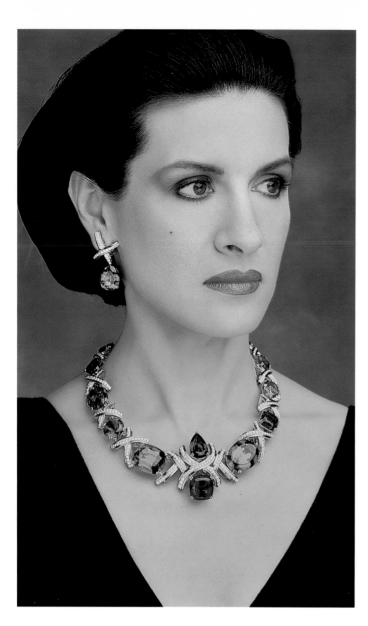

Paloma Picasso

Before joining
Tiffany's design team in
1980, Paloma Picasso
designed costume jewelry for
Yves Saint Laurent in Paris
and gold jewelry for the
Greek firm of Zolotas in
Athens. Her creations are
distinguished by an ample
scale combined with a
boldness and simplicity of
line that have become her
trademark. The necklace
worn by Miss Picasso in this
photograph shows her
fondness for aggressively
stylish color combinations
and simple, linear "X"
patterns.

Collection of Mrs. Paul Hallingby, Jr.

PAGES 184–85
*Tiffany Table Setting, "The
Rich Aunt," 1980s*

Tiffany's table
display shows are an ever
popular attraction of New
York. This Tiffany table is
sumptuously set with Tiffany
Private Stock "Princess
Astrid" dinner plates and
soup dishes. The pattern of
pink and white hawthorn
flowers was specially designed
in Paris by Camille le Tallec
after a Le Tallec dinner
service given to Princess
Astrid of Sweden on her
marriage to Leopold II of
Belgium. "Crysanthemum"
vermeil flatware, and
"Harcourt" crystal by
Baccarat complete the setting.
The delicately hand painted
"Nymphenberg" soup tureen
in the style of Joseph
Zachenberger was made
exclusively for Tiffany's by
Nymphenberg.

RIGHT
Elsa Peretti's Crystal Collection

Accomplished
in the design of crystal as
well as in gold and silver,
Elsa Peretti creates Tiffany
objects whose sensual and
vigorous lines give them both
a forceful presence and a
sense of fluidity. Her "Bone"
candlestick and fishbowl on a
pedestal, like all her
creations, both seduce and
charm.

Acknowledgments

Tiffany & Co. wishes to thank Brad Bealmear; Vivienne Becker; Claude S. Brinegar; Robert Brunet; Carla Capalbo; Charles Carpenter; Stephen Earle; Rita Eckartt; Martin Eidelberg; Suzanne Elrod; R. Esmerian; John Fling; John Funt; David A. Hanks & Associates; Josh Haskin; Debra Healy; Anthony Iorio; Irit Kafkafi; Dr. and Mrs. Michael Kalisman; David Keller; Katherine Kurland; Dimitri Levas; Robert Mehlman; Shelton Mindel & Associates; Lillian Nassau; Henry B. Platt; Penny Proddow; Julie Reisdorf; Dr. and Mrs. Joseph Sataloff; Wendy Umanoff; the late Sam Wagstaff; Bertram Wolfson; Paul Schaffer of À La Vieille Russie; Paul Doros and Jeanne Vibert Sloane of Christie's; Reva Kirschberg of Congregation Emanu-El, New York City; David McFadden of the Cooper-Hewitt Museum, the Smithsonian Institution's National Museum of Design; Charles B. Simmons of the Henry Morrison Flagler Museum; Linda Webb of Thomas J. Lipton, Inc.; Frances Safford of the Metropolitan Museum of Art; Joan Ashley of the Middleborough Historical Musuem; Phyllis Magidson, Margaret D. Stearns, Dr. Deborah Waters of the Museum of the City of New York; Shellie Goldberg of the New York Public Library; Mary De Stafano of the New York Racing Association; Ulysses Dietz of the Newark Museum; David Wright of The Pierpont Morgan Library; John Cherol and Monique Panaggio of The Preservation Society of Newport County; Rev. Monsignor James F. Rigney and Bernie Carroll of St. Patrick's Cathedral, New York City; Ian Irving and Kevin Tierney of Sotheby's.

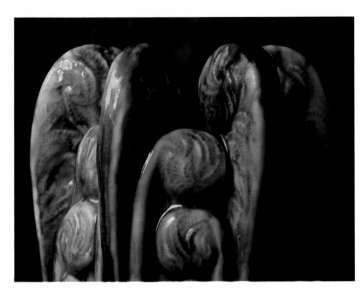

Photography Credits

Jaime Ardiles-Arce: pages 110–11
Billy Cunningham: pages 178, 184–85
Jesse Gerstein: endpapers, pages 2–3, 11, 44–45, 48–49, 50–51, 52, 60–61, 62–63, 64–65, 68, 69, 71 (top), 72, 74, 77, 78 (top), 79, 82, 84, 85, 89, 91, 92, 93, 94–95, 96–97, 98, 99, 104, 108–9, 113, 114, 117, 120, 121, 122–23, 124–25, 126, 127, 128, 132–33, 134, 135, 136, 137, 140, 141, 145, 152, 153, 156, 168, 169, 171, 176, 177, 182–83
Elizabeth Heyert: pages 42, 55, 56, 57, 66, 67, 70, 71 (bottom), 73, 76, 80, 83, 90 (top), 100–1, 106, 107, 112, 115, 150–51, 155, 160
Hiro Studio, Inc.: pages 175, 187
Jeff Hunter: pages 58–59
Kenro Izu: pages 159, 186
Leslie Jean-Bart: page 4
Bill King: page 161
Erik Kvalsvik: page 170
Stephen B. Leek: pages 105, 129, 138–39, 154, 157
Kevin Logan: pages 75, 78 (bottom), 81, 102, 119, 148, 164–65
Sven Martson: page 130

Credits